CW01301856

Online Dating for Men

Discover How to Attract Women and Get a Girlfriend Using the Internet and Dating Apps

© **Copyright 2020**

All Rights Reserved. No part of this book may be reproduced in any form without permission in writing from the author. Reviewers may quote brief passages in reviews.

Disclaimer: No part of this publication may be reproduced or transmitted in any form or by any means, mechanical or electronic, including photocopying or recording, or by any information storage and retrieval system, or transmitted by email without permission in writing from the publisher.

While all attempts have been made to verify the information provided in this publication, neither the author nor the publisher assumes any responsibility for errors, omissions or contrary interpretations of the subject matter herein.

This book is for entertainment purposes only. The views expressed are those of the author alone, and should not be taken as expert instruction or commands. The reader is responsible for his or her own actions.

Adherence to all applicable laws and regulations, including international, federal, state and local laws governing professional licensing, business practices, advertising and all other aspects of doing business in the US, Canada, UK or any other jurisdiction is the sole responsibility of the purchaser or reader.

Neither the author nor the publisher assumes any responsibility or liability whatsoever on the behalf of the purchaser or reader of these materials. Any perceived slight of any individual or organization is purely unintentional

Contents

INTRODUCTION 1
   Consider this *1*
   What it takes to achieve any goal *2*
   The truth about online dating *3*
   The aim of this book and what you will learn *5*
   Before you get started: *6*
SECTION 1 9
CHAPTER 1: THE ULTIMATE GETTING-STARTED GUIDE ... 9
   ONLINE DATING 101: A BRIEF OVERVIEW (OR HISTORY) 12
   HOW ONLINE DATING WORKS 13
      A (very) brief history of online dating *15*
      Significant changes in the 1800s *17*
      The 1900s-date *19*
   THE OUTSTANDING BENEFITS OF ONLINE DATING (WHEN IT'S DONE RIGHT) . 22
   PROS OF ONLINE DATING 22

#: *Easy to get started (fast)* 22

#: *Affordability* 24

#: *Specificity* 25

#: *Ease of creating a connection* 27

#: *Less stressful* 29

#: *Enhanced security* 31

CONS OF ONLINE DATING 34

#: *The paradox of choice* 34

#: *Information limitations* 35

CHAPTER 2: CHOOSING THE BEST DATING WEBSITES AND APPS . 37

#: *Match.com* 38

#: *eHarmony* 39

#: *Elite Singles* 40

#: *OkCupid* 41

#: *Tinder* 43

CHAPTER 3: YOUR PROFILE MATTERS; TIPS FOR AN IRRESISTIBLE ONLINE PRESENCE 47

#: *Your main profile picture is your calling card* 48

#: *Use all your picture slots (and how to do that like a pro)* 50

#: *Show your description/bio some love* 53

#: *Your username matters too* 58

#: *Reel them in with a catchy headline* 58

http://bit.ly/35Qerxt 59

#: *Consistency will get you far* 59

#: *Keep it 100% honest* 59

#: *Grammar and spelling matters* 60

THE 3 MOST LETHAL DATING PROFILE MISTAKES MOST MEN MAKE (AND HOW TO AVOID THEM) 61

#1: *Profile picture mistakes* 61

#2: Description/bio mistakes *62*

#3: Congruency mistakes *64*

SECTION 2 .... **65**

PRIMING YOUR MATCHES, BUILDING ATTRACTION, FLIRTING, PRE-DATING, & WORKING TOWARDS A DATE **65**

CHAPTER 4: FIVE STRATEGIES TO HELP YOU MASTER THE ART OF SENDING FIRST MESSAGES THAT GET RESPONSES **67**

#1: First, put on your spy glasses *68*

#2: "Hi" doesn't cut it *68*

#3: Attentiveness will get you far *69*

#4: You can "novel" your way into her "block list" *70*

#5: Keep it light, fun, flirty, and ongoing *71*

CHAPTER 5: THE LANGUAGE OF FLIRTING: 25 PHRASES WOMEN LOVE **74**

CHAPTER 6: EVERYTHING YOU NEED TO KNOW ABOUT PRE-DATING **82**

#: The Pre-dating phase *82*

#: Pre-dating *84*

CHAPTER 7: THE CREEP FACTOR; HOW TO AVOID BEING MISUNDERSTOOD & OTHER MISTAKES **87**

How to Avoid The "Creep" Label 88

#: Keep it PG13 .... *88*

#: Keep off the sex talk *88*

#: Keep physical-based compliments to yourself *89*

#: Serial texting *89*

#: Over-forwardness *90*

Dating Profile Phrases You Should Not Use 91

#: "Whatever else you want to know, ask." *91*

#: "I recently came out of a relationship." *91*

#: "I love ..." *91*

 #: "I expect you to be ..." 92

 3 ADDITIONAL ONLINE DATING MISTAKES YOU SHOULD AVOID 93

  #: Vague language and generality 93

  #: Using the wrong profile pictures 93

  #: Not messaging enough and messaging too much before setting up a date 93

CHAPTER 8: SCORING A DATE: DOS AND DON'TS 95

  The Dos 95

  The Don'ts 97

CHAPTER 9: THE PERFECT MATCH: 5 SIGNS YOU'VE FOUND YOUR IDEAL PARTNER 99

  #: Consistent communication 99

  #: It's the little things that count 100

  #: Openness 101

  #: You think about her most of the time (if not all the time) 101

  #: You support and encourage each other 101

SECTION 3 103

BEING CONFIDENT AND AWARE WHILE DATING ONLINE 103

CHAPTER 10: ONLINE DATING CONFIDENCE AND HOW TO BOOST IT 104

 WHY CONFIDENCE MATTERS SO MUCH 105

 3 SIMPLE WAYS TO BOOST YOUR DATING CONFIDENCE 106

  #: Cultivate self-awareness 106

  #: Prioritize yourself 106

  #: Swipe, match, message, meet, repeat 107

CHAPTER 11: 3 ONLINE DATING SCAMS AND THE RED FLAGS YOU MUST NEVER IGNORE 108

  #: Phony dating sites 108

  #: The hard come-on 109

  #: Dating bots 109

CHAPTER 12: YOU CAN DO THIS; OVERCOMING ONLINE- DATING HURDLES 111
  Five Single-Parent Dating Hurdles 111
  2: Long-distance Online Romances 113
  3: Unattractive/Not Good-Looking Enough 115
  4: Middle-aged Online Dating Hurdles 117
  How to Overcome Language Barriers in Online Dating......................118
CONCLUSION 119

Introduction

Let me guess; you are reading this book because:

a) You are tired of being single and unsuccessful with women, and because,

b) You want to learn how to use online dating apps and platforms the right way so that you can attract a stunning girlfriend or love partner.

While this undertaking is worthwhile, you need to understand a vital point:

Like most things in life, to master online dating you need the right approach and a fair amount of skill. Without these critical elements that will manifest as excellent interpersonal skills, self-confidence, receptiveness, and a positive attitude, your dating-and-relationship life will continue suffering.

Consider this

The result you want now —and perhaps have always wanted— is *a relationship with a remarkable girlfriend, or to find a life partner – "your person."*

To achieve this result, you are willing to do what it takes, which in this case means mastering online dating and the dating and relationship area of your life. That you have your priorities in order is a good thing.

Now:

To achieve the result and success you want, you need to learn how to navigate the online dating scene like a pro so that you can attract the woman of your dreams.

Unfortunately, a lack of knowledge and confidence, perhaps because of previous online dating failures, mistakes, and misgivings, and the complex nature of online courtships in the modern world have kept you —and are perhaps keeping you—from achieving your chief aim: *a fantastic dating and relationship life!*

Is this relatable?

If it is, before we dig deeper, remember this important point:

What it takes to achieve any goal…

Achieving any goal in life, and yes, attracting women and finding a girlfriend is a goal, depends on two main things: *your intention and motivation.* You need to be intimately aware of your purpose and sure of the motivation behind it.

Only by being sure of these two things will you be willing to do what it takes to achieve your goal. Both of these factors need to have strong rooting in your psyche.

Before we delve deeper into how to use online dating in a way that improves your odds of attracting women and finding a girlfriend, you must clarify your intention and motivation. Having this clarity will significantly improve your overall approach and chances of success.

To clarify the intention and motivation behind your goal, which is *"to use online dating to find an amazing girlfriend,"* you should start by asking yourself the following questions:

- *Are you sick and tired of not knowing what to write on your dating profile, or how to use dating apps and platforms in a way that helps you achieve dating success?*

- *Are you tired of matching with women on Tinder, Match.com, eHarmony, and other online dating platforms, but never knowing what to say to start a conversation that builds attraction and materializes into an offline date?*

- *Are you fed up with using ineffective online dating strategies that take time to implement but that never bear tangible results or work for longer than a few trials or weeks?*

- *Are you finally ready to adopt an online dating approach that, when implemented with diligence and enthusiasm, works as effectively as (or even better than) offline dating?*

If you are, and if you answered yes to at least two of the above questions, you are in luck; you are at the right place because:

The truth about online dating

You see, effective online dating that attracts women and helps you find a girlfriend is not complicated. Matter of fact, using online dating to attract women, find a girlfriend, and improve your dating and relationship life is easier and more fun than you think.

Based on the findings of a 2015 BMJ Evidence-Based Medicine Research study co-authored by Sameer Chaudhry MD., achieving online dating success is a matter of doing two core things:

First, according to the study mentioned above, you need to create a compelling online dating profile. Your online dating profile is the first impression women have of you. If this impression is not stand-out attractive, your profile will suck, and so will your chances of online dating success.

Secondly, after interrogating more than 3,000 studies drawn from fields such as psychology, neurocognitive science, and sociology, Chaudhry et al. concluded that you need to select and approach your matches the right way.

In the modern world, we have dating apps and platforms for all manner of intentions. If you are looking for a "hook up," you will find a dating app or platform for that. If you want female "pen pals", you will find a site or app for that. If you wish to "mingle," you will find an app for that (Mingle2, anyone?)

The dating app you choose to use will significantly impact your chances of finding a girlfriend or romantic partner. It is, therefore, crucial that you go about picking a dating app or platform with care and consideration.

More importantly, no matter which dating app or platform you decide to use, you must approach women in a manner that shows you are authentic and confident, a man worth spending time with and knowing. These research findings should convince you that online dating success is possible for you.

If these findings fail to convince you that you can use online dating to find a girlfriend, the woman of your dreams, or a romantic partner, consider this:

According to a research study published in 2013 by Pew Research, more than half of all online dating interactions —66% to be exact— lead to an actual date. Moreover, according to the data, approximately 23% of online dating interactions that lead to offline dates turn into espousal or long-term relationships.

What does this tell you about online dating?

It should tell you that if you approach online dating the right way and do the right things, you can achieve immense online dating success. Honestly, if you do this thing right, it should be easy to attract women, find a girlfriend, or even meet the woman of your dreams.

You are probably thinking to yourself, *"OK. Now I'm convinced that online dating success is possible. What are the "right things to do" to ensure I achieve online-dating-and-relationship success?"*

Helping you answer that question —and many others like it— is the purpose of this guidebook.

The aim of this book and what you will learn

This book aims to show you the "right things to do" and how to approach online dating in a way that enhances your chances of finding a girlfriend, love, or a long-term partner.

Among many other things, you'll learn:

> • *How online dating works, the various online dating apps and platforms available, and the tools you need to get started. We shall also examine the pros and cons of online dating, the mistakes to avoid, and much more.*

> • *How to become more confident as you navigate through online dating.*

> • *How to cut through the crap, navigate through online dating like a pro, and find love. We'll delve deep into how to choose a dating app or platform suited to your specific dating needs and navigate through it like a seasoned veteran.*

> • *Invaluable, practical tips and strategies you can use to create an irresistible online dating profile that attracts matches, helps you stand out, and that is genuinely you.*

> • *Dating-profile mistakes you should avoid to ensure that women do not misunderstand you or think you are an internet creep.*

> • *The various red flags you should keep in mind to avoid online dating scams.*

- *Spellbinding flirting phrases that women love. Using these phrases with your online matches will help you build palpable chemistry and attraction. With chemistry, rapport, and seduction in play, your online matches will be itching to say yes to your proposal to meet up for coffee, lunch, dinner, or drinks.*

- *The most important signs you should look out for to determine if you have found your ideal match or perfect partner.*

- *The various things to do and steps to take to turn an online match into an offline date. We shall also discuss the biggest mistakes to avoid when working towards scoring an offline date with your matches.*

- *How to overcome various online dating hurdles and solutions to employ when facing varied online dating challenges.*

And much, much more.

As you can see, this book is brimming with invaluable online dating advice and practical strategies.

If you commit to implementing these strategies, you will navigate through online dating like a pro, attract women, and find a girlfriend without much trouble.

Before you get started:

Can you remember what we mentioned about goals and the core ingredients it takes to achieve them? To recap, we noted that achieving goals depends on two main components: *your intention* and *motivation*.

We detailed the questions you need to ask yourself to clarify the intentions and motivation behind your online dating endeavor.

As you move on into the first section and the practical aspects of this book, take a moment to think about why you want a girlfriend. Pay attention to the picture that comes to mind when you think about the girlfriend you want to attract.

Then, cement your intention and motivation for the goal at hand as follows:

Think deeply about attracting the girlfriend of your dreams and visualize how amazing it will feel to be with her and to go out on dates with this incredible woman.

Think of how amazing it will feel when hand-in-hand, you and your girlfriend walk down the street or into weekend barbecues with friends and family. Think of how satisfactory your dating and relationship will be once you master online dating and attract a fantastic girlfriend.

Is this picture clear in your mind? If you have crystallized it, now understand this:

If your intention and motivation are clear, and if you have a burning desire to master online dating and achieve your goal of getting a girlfriend, you will!

Even if you are new to online dating, you can have the life you just imagined. Even if you are the most unconfident, shy man alive, you can attract the woman of your dreams. Even if you have failed at online dating several times before, the woman of your dreams and the life you just imagined can be yours.

Are you eager to know what it will take to become that person and to experience the life you just imagined?

Here it is:

To experience the life you just visualized, all you need to do is to *start implementing the online dating strategies you will learn from this invaluable guidebook!*

Can you do that?

Can you take what you learn from this book and apply it? Can you be open-minded enough to try the various strategies we will discuss in this guide regardless of how unconventional they seem at first?

If you can, and if you are ready and committed to doing what it takes to achieve online dating success, then with this book by your side, without a doubt, you will achieve this success!

Now that you are primed, ready, and pumped to get started, giddy-up to the first section of the guide!

Section 1
The Ultimate Getting-Started Guide

"In its purest form, dating is auditioning for mating (and auditioning means we may or may not get the part)."

Joy Browne

Welcome to the first section of this online dating guidebook for men.

This section will serve as an introductory guide to online dating. In this section, we will cover areas such as:

- *A basic introduction to the state of online dating in the modern world and how online dating works.*

- *The various advantages and disadvantages of online dating and the tools you need to get started.*

- *The available dating apps and platforms and how to choose one specifically suited to your dating needs.*

- *Practical and invaluable tips and strategies you should use to create an irresistible and authentic online dating profile that attracts matches and dates.*

And much, much more.

After reading the various chapters that make up this section of the book, you will have a firm foundation upon which to build your online dating success.

Chapter 1: The Online Dating World; Know Your Stuff

Matchmaking services, which are essentially the fundamental concept behind online dating, are not new.

In a 1992 journal article titled *Formal Intermediaries in the Marriage Market: A Typology and Review*, Ahuvia & Adelman et al. note, *"institutional and human intermediaries in romantic relationships have been part of social interactions for centuries."*

The journal article continues by asserting:

"Traditionally, these matchmaking intermediaries [services] took forms such as blind dates arranged by family and friends, matchmakers, personal advertisements in newspapers and magazines, video dating, and [more recently], speed dating."

What we can glean from the findings of the journal article mentioned above is that online dating is not novel. Matchmaking, an age-old practice, is its foundational principle.

What makes online dating unique is that instead of using the matchmaking intermediaries and methods mentioned above, online dating uses the internet and various technologies to find romantic partners.

Before we move further into the book, we should step back a bit:

Online Dating 101: A Brief Overview (or History)

Online dating, also called *internet dating*, is what the name suggests: *using the internet to foster personal connections and relationships*. It entails using internet-based technologies such as websites and apps to find and interact with new people with the specific purpose of developing romantic or personal relationships.

For interactions that may (or may not) lead to romantic relationships and relational connections, online daters rely on what we call *online dating service (s)*.

By alluding to the journal paper mentioned earlier, we can define online dating services, platforms, and apps as *"intermediaries that facilitate romantic matchmaking services in the 21st century."*

While most of these companies and services have individualized platforms and designs, mechanisms, and matchmaking algorithms, most have a similar format.

On most online dating apps and platforms, you have to become a member by creating a "profile." Creating this profile gives you the ability to upload personal information such as age, gender & sexual orientation, pictures, appearance, interests, and other dating preferences.

Once you create a profile and populate it with relevant personal information such as your romantic interests, the platform(s) use the information to match you to potential mates.

Additionally, on most popular online dating services, platforms, and apps, once you become a member and create a profile, you gain the ability to view other members' profiles. Based on the visible information these members have shared, you can then decide whether a person is an ideal match and whether to initiate contact.

When it comes to initiating contact with potential matches and women you would like to interact with or date, these services offer various options. On most modern online dating services, platforms, and apps, you will have very advanced messaging features and online chat functionalities aimed at helping you remain "digitally safe."

These messaging functionalities make it easier to reach out to your "matches" safely and securely without compromising your sensitive data such as phone number or email address.

In its most basic sense, that's all there is to online dating: you sign up and get started.

How Online Dating Works

You start by becoming a member of a dating service, app, or website by creating a profile that you then populate with personal information. Once you create this profile, the app or platform gives you the ability to view the profiles of other "online daters." You can then use the data uploaded to these online dating profiles to determine which women you like and would like to talk to or meet.

On most modern dating websites and apps such as Tinder, Tagged, Bumble, Jswipe, etc., when you find a woman you think is interesting, you press "YES" or "SWIPE RIGHT" to indicate you would like to talk to or "know her." A "LEFT SWIPE" or "NO" does the opposite: *it shows your disinterest in a particular woman.*

When a woman "SWIPES RIGHT" on you, indicating interest in you or the desire to get to know you better, it becomes a "MATCH." A match illustrates that both parties —the woman and you— find each other exciting enough to want to know more.

This match immediately gives you the ability to reach out to the said woman through the built-in safe-messaging functions. Either party can start a conversation, but the norm is for the man to start the conversation.

Depending on how the conversation begins and unfolds, you can build attraction and rapport. Eventually, you can share personal information such as phone numbers so that you can plan in-person meetups.

Today, online dating services and platforms give you a lot of diversity, flexibility, and functionality. For example, on some platforms, you can view the profile of other online daters before you become a member. On such platforms, once you notice the profile of a woman you would like to contact, you have to create a profile to do so.

Other platforms such as Tinder have membership subscription options whereby you pay a monthly fee. When you pay this fee, you can view the profiles of women who "SWIPE RIGHT" on you without waiting for a match to happen organically. Such a feature is especially useful because, with the option active, you can view the profiles of women that would like to "know you."

Once you see these profiles, you can then determine which of these women you would like to *swipe right* on to create a match. Once a match occurs, you can then start messaging and building the conversation towards an in-person date or pre-date.

The above is all there is to know about what online dating is and how it works.

As implied earlier, your success with online dating hinges on your ability to choose a dating service, app, or platform suited to your dating needs. It also depends on how well you optimize your profile to attract matches.

Various parts of this guide will discuss actionable strategies you can use when deciding which dating app to use and how to optimize your online dating profile.

Before we get to that, we need to briefly discuss how internet dating has evolved, and how our sentiments and psychological biases towards dating in the modern world have changed.

A (very) brief history of online dating

In the Second (2015) Edition of the *International Encyclopedia of the Social & Behavioral Sciences,* Monica T. Whitty, Ph.D., notes that in their most primitive form, online dating sites and platforms started cropping up in the 1980s.

Dr. Whitty goes on to note that in the early days, according to research conducted in 1995 by Scharlott and Christ, online dating attracted stigma, and early internet adopters were somewhat wary of using the internet to find mates or romantic partners.

Today's dating apps and websites are very graphically aesthetic, even beautifully laid out. That was not always the case. In the book mentioned above, Dr. Whitty further notes that in their most primitive form in the 80s, internet-dating sites were mostly text-based, and users intending to create online dating profiles had minimal profile-creation options.

Although we can trace the rise of online dating —as we know it— to the 80s, the 80s is not necessarily when the trend started. Yes, the 80s were pivotal to the development of online dating as we know it today thanks in part to changing sentiments towards courtships and technological advancements such as the personal computer and the internet, but online dating goes back even further.

First personal ad

H.G. Cooks, an Associate Professor of History at Nottingham University, UK, notes that personal ads, which are the foundation upon which online dating is built, started in 1695.

The professor believes that the first personal ad, a solicitation for matrimony, appeared in a British Paper on July 19, 1695.

He further notes that in the early days, personal ads were popular with British men of repute who wanted to find spouses without using the traditional format where family and friends introduced and "set up" bachelors.

Funny personal ads in the 1600s

A visit to modern-day online dating platforms will reveal profiles of online daters poking fun at themselves or online dating.

This modern-seeming trend is as old as personal ads.

16-year-old Benjamin Franklin —not the founding father— was the first to place a "funny" personal ad in the April 23, 1772 publication of *The New England Courant*.

Here is what he wrote as a joke —the joke was on him because he received tons of responses:

> *"Any young Gentlewoman that is minded to dispose of herself in Marriage to a well-accomplished young Widower, and has five or six hundred pounds to secure to him by Deed of Gift. She may repair to the Sign of the Glass-Lanthorn in Steeple-Square, to find all the encouragement she can reasonably desire."*

If you placed such an ad in the paper or used such words to describe yourself on an online dating profile today, many would consider your ad a plea for a "sugar-mama," or rather, a well-off woman who can care for your financial needs.

Well-to-do women (and men) looking for love — mostly from younger men or women — is not a new trend.

A woman places the first personal ad

Many historians believe that Helen Morrison, a lonely spinster, was **the first woman to place a personal ad in the Lonely Hearts Column in 1727.**

The *People Almanac* notes that shortly after her desperate plea moved the editor of the *Manchester Weekly Journal* to publish her ad, she received a response, but not the kind she had hoped for or wanted. The response she received was from the government; the mayor had ordered her committed to an asylum for four weeks.

Early personal ads focused on respect

In the early days of personal ads in newspapers, men were the ones most likely to use the medium. Although personal ads have changed significantly, the basic principles in play then are still somewhat relevant today.

As an example, in the early days of personal ads, the men using these ads to look for spouses had to be very mindful of the wording they used when creating these ads and describing themselves.

In the Victorian era, for example, the focus was on making sure the ads had a dignified and respectable wording and aura. A good example of this is an ad published in an 1851 publication of *The Manchester Guardian*. It read:

"A Gentleman, about 27 years of age, kind and amiable in disposition, is desirous of meeting with a Partner for Life. The advertiser is engaged in a prosperous business; and trusts that this mode may be the means of bringing him into communication with one of the fair sex similarly disposed, and of a respectable family."

The ad received a fair amount of responses from interested women and is a prime example of how having an optimized personal ad description can influence response rates.

These sentiments remain true today with online dating; how you describe yourself determines your "attractiveness" (and hence, your response rate), and is why creating a good online dating profile is so important. We will discuss how to do this later.

Significant changes in the 1800s

In the 1800s, personal ads were much more prevalent, and sentiments towards the idea had started shifting significantly. In this era, the ads become more than about seeking matrimony-driven relationships and courtships. They started becoming a somewhat socially accepted way of meeting potential mates and partners, and as periodicals and magazines become popular, they became more about seeking companionship.

For example, during the American Civil War of the 1800s —and other 18th century wars— Cocks notes that it was common for soldiers to place personal ads in newspapers looking for companionship through pen pals. He goes on to note that even though these ads were widely used, many were still skeptical about them, the probability of scams, and the implications such forms of dating had on social morality.

Speaking of scams:

Early dating scams and "catfishing"

How to stay safe from online dating scams and "catfishers" is an issue we shall discuss at length later in this guidebook.

Online dating scams are not new. As is the case with modern online dating, early personal ads had an element of "risk" in the sense that even in those days, it was possible to fall prey to scams and swindles.

An early example of a personal ad scam appears in a **report published in the New York Times.** The report indicates that in 1897, a young woman named Tillie Marshall placed an ad in which she claimed she was a wealthy widow—wealthy to the tune of $20,000— interested in a life partner.

Many of her male correspondents —and there were plenty— sent her money so that she could travel from San Francisco to meet with them in cities as far away as New York, Washington, and Chicago.

Tillie used the remittances to fund her globe-trotting lifestyle. Before long, she met a foreign "gentleman" who financed her travel to Europe. She left without ever meeting any of the men that had sent her money, and as she "vacationed," through Europe, she continued swindling men out of their money.

Another example of a sadder story of an early dating scam is the story of Reuben Lane. His story relates very significantly to what we now call "catfishing," an instance where men and women create fake dating profiles that they then use maliciously to defraud, cheat, and abuse.

The story unfolds as follows.

In 1897 —coincidentally, the same year Tillie Marshall was running her "game"— with the promise of marriage nestled deep in his heart, Reuben Lane used his crutches to walk from Barnsborough, Pennsylvania, to Topeka, Kansas; the 1104.01-miles journey took him 36 days. Upon arriving, his intended bride, Eliza Parker (a widow twenty-seven years his senior), callously changed her mind, refused him, and sent him packing back home.

Although sad to the core, Reuben's story is very pertinent in today's online dating scene; as you use online dating, be mindful enough to discern the characters of the women with whom you interact.

While "being vulnerable" and pregnant with the longing for love and companionship is a good thing, do not let it blind you to the tell-tale signs of a scam. In a later section of this guide, we shall discuss the signs you should watch for to determine if you have met the woman of your dreams.

The 1900s-date

At the turn of the 19th century, specifically the early 1920s, personal ads became immensely popular in part because World War 1 soldiers were in dire need of pen pals and "friendly correspondents."

The early 1950s and '60s heralded the "free love" movement, and with it, the modern era of online dating. From the 1960s through the 1980s, as social sentiments towards sexuality and marriage started changing, so did the nature of personal ads. Most of the personal ads published in this era were more liberal, and many had an element of *"seeking dates and flings," married women seeking sex, and gays secretly looking to connect with like-minded individuals.*

The introduction of the internet and personal computer in the late 1990s significantly changed personal ads. Instead of placing personal ads in newspapers and magazines, the adopters of the "free love" movement started using websites. Early brick-and-mortar dating agencies started taking form as well.

As these agencies competed for users, their functionalities evolved to keep pace with technological advancements. For instance, some platforms capitalized on the computer craze to create dating algorithms that they would then use to match their subscribers with potential mates —for a fee.

This craze continues to date.

Today

The introduction of advanced website technologies, smartphones, and smartphone apps has enhanced dating in the modern world. Today, online dating is a socially accepted norm that has heralded far-reaching changes and implications on our attitudes towards dating.

Online dating in the modern world is vastly different from its early roots. That said, the primary benefits it gave its users in the early days are still the same benefits driving you and modern users into using the various online dating apps, platforms, and services.

In the early days of personal ads, the benefit or "WHY" driving these personal ads was a desire to meet someone an advertiser would otherwise have not met, for any number of reasons. For instance, in the early days, a farmer living in some remote countryside cottage would place an ad in the local paper hoping to meet a partner.

"Creating a connection" is still the primary factor driving hopeful daters to use online dating; it remains the same reason that motivates people from all walks of life to board the online-dating train. The only things that have changed significantly are the mediums we use to connect with others with romantic interests at heart and the fact that, unlike newspaper and magazine ads, online dating services are far more efficacious and functional.

Now that we have mentioned benefits and functionalities, it is essential to point out that even though online dating has changed significantly over time, you can still place personal ads in newspapers and magazines.

You can do so using the same format used by online-dating adopters of the early 1600s.

Today, the downside to using such ads is that they are not as feature-rich as online dating apps, nor as secure or convenient. For example, if you place a personal ad in the newspaper, other than defining the kind of person you would like to meet, you have no actual control over who reaches out to you. Anyone, even those who do not meet your search criteria, can reach out to you through the connection medium you would have provided.

Moreover, like the ad placed by Tillie Marshall, such ads are treasure troves for "catfishers" and fraudsters. They also put you at risk because you have to give out your contact information such as email or phone number. Publicly sharing sensitive information opens you up to cyberattacks, identity theft, bullying, and in some instances, nuisance communication from women you do not want to date.

Internet or online dating helps you avoid all that.

Online dating services help you define your search criteria more clearly —and therefore eliminate any matches that do not meet your parameters. Moreover, most online dating apps and websites do not require that you share your contact details. Most have sophisticated, built-in messaging tools that you can use to contact your matches without explicitly sharing any personal information.

Online dating has many other advantages over personal ads and conventional dating. Let us discuss these advantages.

The Outstanding Benefits of Online Dating (When it's Done Right)

Online dating has many benefits; no one can dispute that, especially when we consider the at-the-click-of-a-button convenience and variety it has given us.

With that noted, like most useful things in life, online dating also has its fair share of disadvantages. Although the discussion we shall carry on in this subsection will concentrate on the benefits of online dating, we will also discuss its disadvantages (or cons). Doing otherwise would be a disservice to you.

Let us start with the advantages:

Pros of Online Dating

On a post published on the MTV news page, Arabelle Sicardi, notes, *"[...online dating has done more than change how we meet others; it has designed it entirely...]."*

That is true: online dating has changed our perception towards dating and courtships so significantly that, according to statistics published by eHarmony, as much as 20% of all current long-term relationships started online.

The list below outlines the most notable benefits of online dating.

#: Easy to get started (fast)

We talked a bit about how online dating started in the 1600s in the form of personal ads. We also mentioned that even though very few people do it now, you can still place personal ads in local newspapers and magazines.

What makes online dating superior —and why you should go the online dating route instead of the personal ad route— is that getting started is extremely easy. All you have to do is navigate to a dating page or install a dating app on your phone, create a profile and populate it with relevant information, perhaps pay for a subscription—depending on the platform you are using— and voila: you are ready to get started!

The fact that you can create a profile so straightforwardly and so fast, coupled with the fact that online dating sites and apps are so accessible, makes online dating superior to all other forms of meeting new people offline.

Consider this:

To place a personal ad in the local paper, you have to go to their offices, write what you want the ad to say on a piece of paper (keeping in mind the word count), and then pay for the commercial; altogether, this process can take several hours.

Online dating is different in the sense that all you have to do is navigate to a dating platform, create your profile, and in most cases, immediately start browsing through dating profiles and matching with women you would like to meet.

Getting started fast is an especially good thing when you lack dating confidence; when starting is easy, you are unlikely to overthink the process or experience "analysis paralysis".

On some dating applications/platforms such as Tinder, you do not even have to populate your profile; you can connect it with your social media accounts such as Facebook and Instagram and automatically have the app fill your profile with relevant information and pictures.

You can get started fast, yes, but to enhance your chances of finding a girlfriend and perhaps love through online dating, you need to pay special attention to your profile and create it in a way that helps you communicate that you are authentic and deeply invested in finding someone genuine and interested in the same thing you are: *a boyfriend-girlfriend relationship.*

#: Affordability

To understand how immensely affordable online dating is, we need to compare it to personal ads and using offline means to meet new women.

As mentioned, to place a personal ad in a newspaper or magazines, you need to make your way to their offices, spend a few minutes — or perhaps more than a few minutes— creating an optimized ad, and then pay for the ad that, in most cases, is charged according to the number of words you use.

With this avenue, the first thing you have to do is travel to the offices of the newspaper or magazine in which you want to place the advertisement, which costs money in fuel or a bus pass. More importantly, it takes time, and as you know, time is an invaluable resource whose worth we cannot quantify.

Using offline means to meet women by visiting the local bar, festivals, etc., also has attendant costs. First, you have to make your way to these locations, which, even if it does not require some form of transportation, costs time.

Secondly, once you are at that bar or festival, you have to pay some form of entrance fee and in the case of a bar, you have to buy drinks and perhaps food as you bide your time looking for a woman you can approach.

These costs can add up to a pretty penny, especially when you take to going out several times a week. The sad truth is that doing all this does not guarantee that you will meet a compatible woman and develop a relationship.

Online dating does not have any of the above shortcomings or attendant costs —at least not initially. As mentioned previously, to get started on most dating platforms all you have to do is create a profile. This profile then gives you access to the dating profiles of millions of users, all at the click of a button.

Moreover, even in instances where a dating site requires a subscription, the subscription fee is so small compared to placing personal ads or using offline means to meet women, that online dating is far more affordable.

Match.com and eHarmony.com, two of the most popular subscription-based dating sites in the U.S., have a monthly subscription of $42 and $60, respectively.

In comparison:

In the U.S. and UK, the average cost of a meal at a restaurant or club is $7, and the cost of drinks is $3 for a beer, $6 for cocktails, and $10 for any of the fancier drinks. Conservatively, if you visit the local bar three times a week looking for the girlfriend of your dreams, and have one meal and three beers per visit, you will have spent at least $96 at the end of the month, and this is minus the additional sums you direct towards "entertaining" the women you meet by buying them drinks and meals.

Without a doubt, even when you factor in the cost of a subscription, online dating is way, way cheaper. The cost lowers further when you consider that on most dating platforms, a paid membership is optional, and even without it, you still have access to the dating profiles of millions of users whom you can match with and start chatting.

NOTE: On most dating platforms, premium memberships give you access to advanced features. For instance, on Tinder, a subscription allows you to view the women that "liked" or clicked "yes" on you and to expand your search criteria to other countries.

#: Specificity

Specificity is perhaps one of the most marked benefits of online dating. To comprehend just how immensely specific online dating allows you to be with what you want, we need to juxtapose it against meeting new women offline and placing personal ads.

When you place a personal ad in the local paper or magazine, you can define the type of woman you want, her interests, looks, and the likes. The same principle applies to meeting women offline; you are at liberty to decide which women to approach —or not to approach— depending on what you see or intuit.

However, with both options, there are no guarantees that the person you meet will have similar interests or the core character traits you want in a long-term girlfriend. With personal ads, the issue is worse because once you give out your contact details, you have no control over who can contact you; even women who fail to match your search criteria can contact you with unwanted messages and propositions.

No doubt, meeting women offline can be exciting, but because you are taking a chance on someone new, and because people rarely project their genuine self initially, it is tough to determine if a woman you want to approach or if a woman you end up approaching has the character traits you consider essential in a girlfriend or long-term partner.

Online dating eliminates the "shot-in-the-dark" aspect of dating.

When creating an online dating profile, the first thing you do is define the kind of person you want. For instance, you can set your search criteria to "*women, aged between 20-35, within a 10mile radius.*" This option alone gives you a level of specificity you cannot have when using offline means to meet people or by placing personal ads.

Moreover, once you create a profile, the platform uses the information you provide in your profile to match you to potential mates. For instance, once you fill out what you are "looking for," your likes and interests, hobbies, and the like, the platform uses its dating algorithm to match your dating profile to that of others users who may have similar interests or who may have used related words to describe themselves.

Most dating platforms take this specificity a bit further. For instance, on Match.com and eHarmony, you have to fill out a lengthy questionnaire. This questionnaire is essential because it allows the dating algorithm to match you to compatible mates and women with interests similar to yours.

On some dating platforms, you can go as far as defining whether you would like to meet a smoker or non-smoker, religious or non-religious, and even someone who has specific political views. For instance, if you are a big supporter of Bernie Sanders, you can try Bernie's Singles. On the other hand, if you want to meet a Christian woman, there is Christian Mingle. If you like fitness, you can use Fitness Singles to meet a woman interested in fitness. If you want to meet a well-off woman, you can use Millionaire Match.

Online dating is so specific that you can even specify the kind of woman you want to meet based on ethnicity —dating sites such as Interracial Cupid, Thai Cupid, and Afro Introductions are prime examples.

With online dating, you are free to be as specific as you want without feeling as if you are too demanding because unless you give someone access to your profile's backend, no one can ascertain the search parameters you have in place.

NOTE: Even though you should be very specific about the kind of girlfriend you want, being open-minded and ready to meet all types of women will significantly enhance your chances of meeting and starting a relationship with a woman that blows your mind.

#: Ease of creating a connection

If you have ever tried offline dating, you know that the thought of walking up and starting a conversation with a woman you have never met before can be nerve-wracking. Fears related to "What do I say?" and "What if I make a fool of myself?" are usually the primary hindrances to meeting and approaching new people.

While the fear of "what to say" seeps into online dating as well, it is not as pronounced as it is when meeting people offline. Part of the reason for this has to do with the fact that in most instances, online daters share a lot of information about themselves.

For example, a woman may share what she likes doing in her free time, what she does career-wise, the kind of person she wants to connect with, and other such relevant information.

That online daters typically share so much information about themselves is a good thing because it makes starting a conversation and creating a connection with a woman relatively easy.

Take an instance where a woman's profile indicates that she likes weekend road trips, camping, listening to music, and reading. If you have similar likes, or if one of your likes aligns with hers, starting a conversation becomes a simple matter of saying hello, introducing yourself, and then using your mutual interests to create a genuine connection.

Having access to information such as what a woman likes before you reach out to her goes beyond making it easier to cultivate a genuine connection. It also allows you to "click yes" or to choose to match with women that interest you.

If you dislike the beach —yes, it is possible to hate the beach— you can avoid matching with women who have sentiments such as *"I live for the sand, sun, and surf"* on their dating profile and instead connect with women who have interests similar to yours —women who like hiking, for example.

Matching with women with whom you have common interests makes starting conversations more natural and comfortable. It also makes it likelier that once the conversation begins, keeping it going, and moving it towards an offline date will come more naturally because all there is to do is to use your mutual interests as a springboard to discover more about each other and to build rapport and mutual attraction.

#: Less stressful

Meeting women offline —perhaps at the library, bars, festivals, etc. — can be very stressful because of several factors.

First, you have to be very mindful of your outer appearance; you have to think about what to wear, you have to bear in mind that in addition to being genuine and authentic, you also have to present yourself in a confident way that portrays you as an ideal catch.

Secondly, as mentioned earlier, meeting and approaching women offline has an element of stress and anxiety because you have to worry about what to say and how to contact these women in a confident as well as respectful manner. Striking this balance can add to the stress.

Online dating takes away most of this pressure, again, because of various reasons:

The first thing worth noting is that while you should ensure that your online conversations build to offline dates, there are no explicit rules that every conversation you have with every woman you meet online should lead to a date or a relationship.

In fact, a large percentage of conversations started on online dating platforms do not materialize into anything substantive, which is OK. Knowing that not every conversation you start with women will lead to anything substantive is enough to ease the stress and anxiety often attached to the process of introducing yourself to someone new in a manner that creates immediate attraction.

Secondly, as mentioned earlier, unlike offline dating where you know very little about the women you approach, in online dating, you know quite a lot about your matches. You also have control over which women you match with, which in addition to giving you an immense amount of control, also eliminates a great deal of the stress attached to first introductions.

Moreover, the differences between starting an online and in-person conversation are very stark. In in-person conversations, the fact that you are in the woman's vicinity means your body language will be clear for her to read, which means if you are nervous or anxious, it will be clear for her to see, which will influence your chances with her, and add a lot of pressure to the undertaking.

When starting online conversations, such is not the case. For one, you are using messages to connect. Online messages do not have an element of body language; all you have to worry about is the tone of your messages and the sentiments you communicate, a relatively easy thing to do.

Online messaging also has an innate degree of impersonality. For instance, flirting in person is very challenging; in comparison, flirting over text messages is relatively easy to pull off even if you are new to it or shy and unconfident.

Online dating eases dating stress and anxiety in another critical way. Most online dating platforms have features such as "sending love," "super likes," "commenting on photos," "liking a profile," "super liking," etc. These low-key ways of showing interest in a woman are incredible because they allow you to be a bit "covert" with your interest in her.

The fact that you can "send a woman love", "super like her," or comment on her profile or profile picture makes it easier to gauge her interest in you before you open a conversation. If she responds in kind, you can rest assured that starting a conversation will lead to a response that can remove a lot of the angst attached to reaching out to new people.

#: Enhanced security

Can you remember the story of Tillie Marshall —we discussed it earlier and said it was the earliest form of online dating scam?

Online dating largely eliminates such elements.

Consider the idea of placing a personal ad in the local paper or magazine. With such an option, to ensure potential matches reach out, you have to provide some way for them to contact you; in most cases, you give out your phone number or your email address.

Such a condition is risky because we live in the age of cyber-threats, identity theft, and unsolicited cold calls. Publicly giving out your email is especially unsafe because hackers can send you spam emails that install malware on your computer or phone and steal sensitive data. Giving out your phone number to the world is no better.

If we move away from personal ads, we can also say that meeting strangers offline at bars or other such places is not exactly safe. For starters, when you decide to approach a woman, you have no idea who she is; for all you know, you could be approaching a serial killer, a psychopath, or the leader of a terrorist cell.

Additionally, we live in an age where women carry pepper spray, stun guns, and other weapons in their handbags, and are not afraid to use them when they feel a tiny bit threatened. While your intention is not to approach a woman in a threatening way, there is no telling which approaches a woman may consider threatening.

While online dating has had its fair share of scary stories, scams, and even scandals, the overall consensus is that it is safer than meeting strangers offline —at least at first.

Part of the reason for this is because, for starters, most online dating profiles do not require you to share sensitive information such as your email or phone number publicly. Instead, they offer advanced messaging capabilities that you can use to communicate with your matches. You can then use the nature of your communication to determine whether you would like to share additional contact information.

The other reason why online dating is more secure has to do with the fact that before you start conversations with strangers or share your information with them, you can use the information they have shared on their profile to vet them.

Another important thing worth noting is that most of the popular dating apps have enhanced security features whose purpose is to ensure the safety of their users. For instance, most of these platforms have built-in scammer filtering and protection features, two-factor authentication to ensure no other person can gain access to your profile, and other features such as the ability to block "nuisance" users.

In some cases, dating sites will ask for identity verification; some exclusive dating platforms go as far as doing a background check and having an in-house moderator team that removes fake profiles. Together, these features ensure that as you use online dating, you can rest easy in the knowledge that your information is as safe as it can be anywhere.

#: *Convenience*

This advantage has to do with time.

One of the many things we have noted about meeting new women offline or placing ads in the paper or magazine is that in addition to being costly, it is time-consuming. If we use the example of placing an advertisement in the paper again, we see that in addition to the payment you have to make to ensure the newspaper publishes your ad, you also have to go to their offices.

Likewise, when it comes to meeting women offline, in addition to the astronomical costs we mentioned earlier related to meals and drinks, you also have to dedicate a fair amount of time to the venture, time you could otherwise spend on self-improvement and turning yourself into the best man possible —and guess what, women love men who dedicate themselves to personal development.

At first, online dating does not require an astronomical amount of time. In fact, many men do it —and do it well for that matter— in as little as 15 minutes a day.

With online dating, you do not have to worry yourself to death —at least not at first— with time-consuming things such as where to go, what to dress in, what to say, where to park once you get to the venue, etc. All you have to do is sign up, populate your profile with relevant information, and then spend a few minutes of your day swiping or communicating with your matches.

Moreover, the fact that you can chat with women from all over the world from the comfort of your home, while sitting on the toilet bowl, eating, watching TV, after work, etc. is convenient.

Yes, once you start chatting with an interesting woman you would like to meet, you will have to think about where to take her, what to dress in, mode of transportation, and other such things, but initially, you do not have to worry about such pressure. All you have to do is enjoy the process.

The above are the most outstanding benefits of online dating. This list does not even come close to detailing all the benefits of online dating. Some of the other benefits we did not mention here include things like the fact that online dating eliminates the embarrassment of rejection, is a great deal of fun, and is very successful when done right —don't let the critics fool you: online dating works when you work it!

These benefits should serve to motivate you and show you that when you approach online dating the right way, in addition to accruing these benefits, you can also find immense success.

As mentioned at the start of this chapter, just as most good things in life have a downside, online dating has its shortcomings. While these weaknesses cannot overpower the benefits, failing to mention them will be a disservice to you because once you become aware of these shortcomings, it will be easier to see some of the mistakes you need to avoid to achieve online dating success.

Here are the most marked disadvantages of online dating:

Cons of Online Dating

Before we start talking about the challenges of online dating, you should keep it in mind that the aim of looking at these disadvantages is not to discourage you. If we were to juxtapose the cons against the pros, the pros would come out winners in every bout.

As stated earlier, the aim of highlighting these cons is to give you awareness, so that you can go into the venture well-prepared.

Since we have that out of the way, here are the disadvantages of online dating —at least the ones you should be aware of for now:

#: The paradox of choice

One advantage of online dating is that it gives you a truckload of options. Think of it this way.

According to data from Statista, as of April 2017, as much as 19% of U.S. internet users are using at least one dating website or app. Given that the U.S. Census Bureau indicates that as much as 78% of the population has access to the internet, we are talking about millions and millions of dating options available to you at the click of a button.

To quantify this, data published on datingsitesreviews.com, the U.S has about 59 million online dating users. 40% of these are women; men make up the remaining 60%. Most of these 50+ million users use at least two dating services or apps. What does this tell you?

It should tell you that once you board the online-dating train, choices will inundate you left, right, and center. Once you start using online dating, you will, at one point or the other, experience the paradox of choice.

The fact that you have access to hundreds of thousands of potential matches and dates is good and bad in the same breath.

According to various bodies of research, when we have too many choices, making decisions becomes challenging. In his groundbreaking book, *The paradox of choice: Why more is less*, Stuart B. Schwartz, a Professor of History at Yale University, notes that *"when we have too many choices, we are likely to feel less satisfied with any choice we make."*

Having too many choices can feel overwhelming and cause a lot of anxiety —because of the fear of making the wrong choice. As you navigate the online dating world, you have to be very mindful of this principle. If you are not conscious of it, the sheer number of available and potential matches and dates can overwhelm you to the point of paralysis, a condition that is especially true when you have a well-optimized dating profile that attracts many matches per day.

The online dating seas are abundant, yes, but remember that even the fisherman who goes out to sea does not go out intending to catch every fish in the ocean. He goes out meaning to haul-in a specific amount of "catch" for the day.

To avoid the paradox of choice, apply a similar mentality by defining the type of woman or "catch" you want. Doing this will ensure that when you cast your net, you do not catch too many fish and that when you do, you can "quickly release" any "metaphorical fish" you did not want to "capture" in the first place or that you "cannot eat."

#: Information limitations

In 2012, Finkel et al. published a paper titled, *Online Dating: A Critical Analysis From the Perspective of Psychological Science*. From their research, the authors noted that most online dating profiles lack essential information necessary to determine if one is an ideal match. The authors further stated that such information is more accessible when meeting people offline, and because these online profiles lack this vital information, it is thus far more difficult for online daters to discern compatibility before the first meeting.

These research findings make a lot of sense when you consider the nature of the information uploaded to online dating platforms. For instance:

In a research paper published in 2008 by Frost et al., the researchers noted that most online daters upload information relative to their educational background, physical attributes, and income or work-related undertakings. The researchers further note that this diminishes the efficacy of online dating because the information uploaded does not give potential matches an idea of what it may be like to interact or be with the person.

Moreover, one thing you will quickly notice once you create your online dating profile is that most people tend to embellish. While there is nothing wrong with putting your best foot forward, the fact that online dating profiles often seem to display —to the point of advertising—someone's "better traits" means that the initial connections you create with women will not have a firm footing because, in truth, women (and men for that matter) can populate their profiles with fictitious information meant to paint them in the best possible light.

In the next chapter, we shall discuss various dating apps/platforms so that you can choose one specifically suited to your dating needs.

Chapter 2: Choosing the Best Dating Websites and Apps

We have talked a bit about the evolution of online dating and its effect on the ways we create romantic partnerships, as well as how it has changed our collective psychology towards how modern relationships start.

As we mentioned earlier, in the 1980s, the first dating websites were text-based and very rudimentary. That is no longer the case.

Technological advancements such as smartphones, smartphone apps, and other web-based technologies have made it easier for graphic designers, web developers, and programmers to create intuitive and sophisticated dating apps and websites, and platforms that bring online dating to life.

Today, thanks to those technological advancements, the over 8000 available dating platforms and apps are so feature-rich that as you get started one of the issues you will have to grapple with is that of deciding which app to use.

The less time you spend choosing which dating app to use, the more time you can spend "swiping," matching, talking to women, building attraction, and working towards a date so that you can find yourself a girlfriend.

In an endeavor to make your decision easier, this chapter aims to help you decide which dating app or platform to use so that you can get started as fast as possible.

The list below outlines the best dating platforms of 2020 as well as a small description of the platform, its ideal audience —who should use it— and its advantages and disadvantages.

#: Match.com

https://www.match.com/

Launched in 1995, Match.com is one of the oldest and most well-known online dating platforms. The platform is *excellent for beginner and first-timers because of its ease of use and feature-rich nature.*

Like most modern dating platforms, Match.com also has a smartphone app in addition to the website.

To get started on Match.com, you need to sign up and create a profile. During the signup and profile-creation process, the platform takes you through a questionnaire that asks you to answer questions about your physical attributes, lifestyle habits, hobbies and interests, values, spirituality, salary, etc.

If you do decide to use Match.com, you should answer these questions as honestly as possible because the platform uses this information to pair you with ideal matches.

Once you create a profile, you can use the website or app to swipe left or right (to say yes or no to other online daters.)

The pros

Match.com's most outstanding features are the timeline feature that you can use to "update your status" and the fact that the platform organizes group meetups such as cocktails, bowling, and other types of activities where members can meet and mingle. Being one of the oldest and still one of the most favored, match.com is continually innovating and evolving.

The cons

Match.com has one main disadvantage.

Even though you can create a free profile and use the app to swipe left or right, once you match with women, messaging them requires that you purchase a subscription package. The platform has two types of subscriptions: a standard and premium package

A monthly match.com subscription starts at $35.99, but you can save on the cost by buying a standard or premium, bundled, three, six, or twelve-month subscription plan. A standard three-month bundled subscription costs $19.99 per month.

#: eHarmony

https://www.eharmony.com/

eHarmony launched on August 22, 2000, and is one of the most comprehensive dating platforms available. The platform clearly states that its *ideal user is someone looking for love, a meaningful connection, or a long-term relationship*.

The pros

The most outstanding benefit of using eHarmony is that it has one of the most thorough sign-up processes and dating experiences available on any online dating platform. The profile creation and onboarding process can take as much as 20 minutes.

Like match.com, the profile creation-process has a questionnaire that asks baseline questions about your lifestyle, salary, sexual orientation, likes and dislikes, religious inclination, your self-image, personal beliefs, and values, and what you are looking for in a partner.

Again, if you decide to sign up to eHarmony, be very thorough and honest as you answer the onboarding questionnaires because how well you answer the questions will help you find compatible partners.

The cons

Like match.com —and various other dating platforms— creating a standard account on eHarmony is free. However, without a subscription, you cannot see your matches, the messages they send you, or send them messages either.

The platform does not have a month-to-month subscription. Instead, it has a tiered membership option that starts at $32.95 per month for the three-month subscription:

#: Elite Singles

https://www.elitesingles.com/

Elite Singles describes itself as *"one of the best dating sites for educated singles."* As you can guess, this means the site is <u>ideal for you if you are 30+ years, and your purpose is to meet other academics for a serious relationship</u>—as much as 80% of the site's users are academics.

The pros

Like match.com and eHarmony, the onboarding and profile-creation process at EliteSingles features an in-depth questionnaire you should complete mindfully and honestly so that you can enhance your chances of matching up with ideal partners.

Some of the questions relate to your physical attributes; others refer to how you would describe yourself, the state of your rooms and spaces, your temperament on a scale, and various other questions related to your personality.

These questions, and others about how you would describe your ideal mate, the qualities you consider most important in a mate/relationship, the value you place on physical appearance, etc. comprise the onboarding process which takes approximately 25-minutes. This means the women EliteSingles matches you with will have a very high probability of being ideal mates.

One advantage of using EliteSingles is that at the end of the questionnaire process, you gain access to your personality test, and more importantly, the ability to match with women and to send them "smiles."

The cons

A primary disadvantage of using Elite Singles is that access to some features requires a subscription. For instance, even though the free membership gives you your personality test results and matches count, you cannot see their photos, only their profile information. Moreover, a free account denies you the ability to receive or send messages.

The platform has three membership levels. The standard membership gives you access to messaging features and the ability to view your matches

Pricing for this membership starts at $57.95 for a three-months subscription:

The premium membership gives you access to better features such as unlimited messaging, the ability to view all profiles and photos, and "read receipts" for messages. The premium membership has three levels that start at $32.95 for a 3-month subscription to $22.95 for the 12-month subscription:

#: OkCupid

https://www.okcupid.com/

Launched on January 19, 2004, OkCupid is an intuitive, modern dating platform that has a very fluid site design. Because of its young nature —compared to older dating sites such as Match.com— the platform is *ideal for you if you are a millennial*; it can also work well for you if you are, as the site describes it, *"looking to find love and happiness by creating meaningful connections."*

The pros

One of the advantages of using OkCupid is that even though the profile-creation process has a questionnaire, the onboarding process is fun in the sense that the platform asks "fun" questions, and is not as time-consuming as that of eHarmony, Elite Singles, or Match.com.

Secondly, creating a profile gives you access to the ability to view the profiles of other users and to message them without necessarily purchasing a subscription. The site and app are also straightforward to use.

Thirdly, the app/website has a message filtration feature. This feature ensures that the only messages you receive and can see are from profiles you liked — a very nifty feature considering that messaging does not require a subscription, and any OkCupid user can, therefore, send you a message.

The site and app also use the "swiping system," but unlike other dating apps such as Tinder, the profiles you swipe on have more information since the onboarding process requires the creation of detailed user bio. The user bios are a nice touch because when you match with a woman, the platform displays a percentage scale showing how compatible you are with the person based on how you both answered the onboarding questions.

The cons

The downside to using OkCupid is that because the site is mainly free to use, anyone can sign up —even scammers and people who are not truly serious about dating or finding an ideal partner— a factor that makes finding a serious match less probable.

Moreover, while we can consider the dating platform free-to-use, access to some advanced features require a paid membership. For instance, to access features such as read receipts and the ability to view who "liked you", you need a paid membership.

The platform has a dynamic, two-tiered subscription: a Basic A-List and a Premium A-List.

NOTE: The subscription structure varies from one individual to the next and often depends on factors such as age, gender, location, etc.

#: Tinder

https://tinder.com/

According to data collected by AppAnnie in 2017, Tinder is one of the most popular dating apps and platforms. It also takes home the crown for being the dating app that popularized the "swiping" system now used by most dating apps and platforms.

Tinder is very diverse; *it can work for you irrespective of whether you want a short or long-term relationship, or whether you want to "hook up" or "date casually" as you work towards finding an ideal partner.*

The pros

Tinder's most outstanding feature is that it makes meeting, matching, interacting with, and messaging new women fun and seamless. Being the most well-known "swiping-based dating app," using Tinder is straightforward to the point of making the app feel like a "dating game."

The other thing worth noting about Tinder is that unlike most of the other dating apps and platforms we have discussed thus far, the signup process is dummy-easy.

For starters, Tinder does not have a lengthy questionnaire. All it requires is that you sign up by creating a profile — and, as we shall explain shortly, even that is not necessary. If you do not want to create a profile, you can use your Facebook account to sign up and sign in.

Once you create your profile, the next step is to populate it with a bio/tagline, and to set up your discovery settings —your search radius, whether you are looking for a man or woman, and the age of the person you want.

Tinder is a location-based dating app. As such, once you signup, the app will use your location to match you to women within your search radius, which is an advantage. For instance, you can "tell" Tinder that you want to pair with women within a 10-mile radius of your location, aged between X and Y. This feature makes Tinder very useful because once you match with a woman within your search radius, setting up a date becomes easy since you are in the same locale.

The other advantage of using Tinder is that the only people that can message you —and that you can message— are your matches, which helps eliminate spam messages.

The cons

A primary disadvantage of using Tinder relates to the "swiping" culture and the app's appearance-based nature. Tinder is a picture-based dating profile where you click "yes" or "no" on pictures of women you would or would not like to meet. This nature gives Tinder a "willow" vibe because physical attraction is not enough to gauge romantic compatibility.

This "game-like" aspect of the dating app, coupled with the fact that other than someone's physical appearance you have very little information from which to determine optimal compatibility, makes finding a mate a somewhat shot-in-the-dark undertaking. You will especially become aware of this shortcoming when you start using the app and find yourself struggling with beginning and maintaining conversations with women you matched with solely because you found them physically attractive.

Moreover, the fact that anyone can upload a fake profile picture —or use Google-searched images— to populate a profile increases the chances of catfishing, scams, and identity theft.

The other disadvantage is that Tinder can be very, very addictive in part because of the game-like nature of meeting new women/people. According to statistics published on The Independent, men spend an average of 85 minutes a day on Tinder. The app's time-consuming nature is something you have to be intimately aware of if you decide to use Tinder as your default dating app.

The other thing worth noting is that although Tinder is free-to-use, it limits the number of swipes you have per day. You also need a subscription to gain access to some features. For instance, without a paid subscription, you cannot see who "liked" you, change your location, "undo" a mistake swipe, or "super like" other profiles since the platform gives you just one "super like" every twenty-four hours.

Tinder has two subscription plans: *Tinder Plus* and *Tinder Gold*. Tinder Plus costs $10 per month. Tinder gold costs $14 per month. Both plans have 3, 6, and 12-months bundled cost-saving plans.

The five dating apps/platforms we have discussed in this chapter are the best, most used/popular dating apps; their popularity is likely to increase in 2020 and beyond —especially Tinder.

Now that you know about these popular dating apps, their ideal target audience, advantages, and disadvantages, remember that you can create a dating profile on each of these dating websites/apps. However, for the best results, it is best to concentrate your efforts on one dating app/platform.

Use the information you have learned from this discussion to choose a dating app/platform that is most convenient for you, and that you think enhances your chances of finding an ideal girlfriend.

NOTE: Most of the online dating platforms we have discussed here —and most others— have a basic free option and a subscription-based option. Whether you end up paying for a subscription will largely depend on how motivated you are to find a girlfriend and the dating app you choose to use.

If you choose to use a platform such as Match.com or eHarmony, keep in mind that viewing your matches' profiles and messaging them will require a subscription. With such platforms, makes sure you weigh the pros —enhanced matches with women you are likely to hit it off with— against the cons —the fee.

With free-to-use apps such as Tinder and OkCupid, the trade-off is that because such sites are free, they have very, very many users and, therefore, stiff competition.

Regardless of which dating platform you decide to use, one of the essential things you have to do to ensure online dating success is to create a banging profile that stands out, and that helps you attract matches.

The next chapter gives you invaluable tips and strategies that will help you do this with ease.

Chapter 3: Your Profile Matters; Tips for an Irresistible Online Presence

Throughout our discussions thus far, we have noted that although most online dating platforms have different onboarding processes and questionnaires, the one thing they all have in common is that to get started, you need to create a dating profile.

How you create and fill out this profile is vital, especially on dating platforms such as match.com, OkCupid, Elite Singles, and others where the onboarding questionnaire is integral to the platform's ability to match you with "probable" life-long mates.

Think of it this way:

If we compared online dating to traditional personal ads, then your online dating profile is the advertisement you create to ensure that you attract matches. It is akin to your calling card, and because it is your first contact with potential matches, you have to create it with authenticity, yes, but also in a way that ensures you put your best foot forward.

This chapter aims to give you invaluable strategies, tips, and hacks you can use to create an online dating profile that is genuinely you, and that is also irresistible to women —so much so that they feel compelled to message you first.

NOTE: Implement as many of these strategies and tips as you can but remember that the most important thing is to get started. Overthinking things will lead to analysis paralysis.

#: Your main profile picture is your calling card

No matter how amazing a profile bio or tagline you write, if you fail to give your main profile picture some well-deserved attention to ensure it is irresistible, you will be dooming yourself to online dating purgatory and failure. You need to understand the importance of your primary profile picture.

Once you upload your profile picture, it goes into a sort of "Rolodex." Women and potential matches will then cycle through this "Rolodex" of online dating profiles looking for the "business card" of the man they want to date and/or "start a committed relationship."

Because of this aspect, your main profile picture is very much like the most eye-catching element of a business card. Your bio and profile information act as the contact information you would expect to see when a business card within a Rolodex is interesting enough to warrant a further interrogation.

While your bio and tagline are essential, and you should optimize them —we shall look at how to do that shortly—, your main profile picture is your first point of contact and the first thing women will use to determine if they should swipe left or right on you. You want to ensure that your main profile picture sparks interest.

Yes, that little thumbnail picture is that important, and if you want more matches and more dates, you have to make sure your main profile picture gets women curious enough to want to read your bio or to look over your profile information.

When deciding which image to use as your primary profile picture, you need to pay special attention to several things:

Say cheese

The best way to ensure your dating profile has an attractive profile picture is to make sure that you smile warmly and openly at the camera. According to data analyzed by Zoosk, having a primary profile picture where you are smiling warmly and invitingly at the camera can increase your matches and messages rate by up to 46%.

Show your face

If you follow the first tip above, you should have no problem here. With that note, make sure your primary profile picture clearly shows your face. Avoid using a primary profile picture where you are wearing sunglasses or a hat, group photos, or any other image that does not reveal your features. Having a primary profile picture where you are hiding your face and eyes gives the impression that you are deceitful or trying to hide something –a guaranteed turn-off for most women.

Seek help

Your primary profile picture should communicate three things: *ATC, attractiveness (A), trustworthiness (T), and competence (C)*. According to research, the best way to choose a primary profile picture that embodies these three traits is to have someone else — preferably someone who does not know you very closely/personally— select the image for you because as research has noted, a stranger is likely to notice things about your face you rarely see because your face is so familiar.

Follow Vida's four rules

Vida Select is an online matchmaking firm that has a team of dedicated matchmakers that help clients optimize their online dating profiles. The enterprise continually conducts online dating research studies. Regarding the best way to ensure your primary picture attracts matches and messages, Vida Select advises that you should follow four simple rules:

- Use a high contrast photo
- Use an image where you are the center of attention
- Use a simple but high-quality picture
- Avoid pictures that used the "camera's flash" because it makes you look older

If you pay particular attention to these simple tips, it should be easy to choose the main profile picture that hits the sweet spot.

While we are on the subject of pictures:

#: Use all your picture slots (and how to do that like a pro)

Most online dating apps or platforms allow you to upload 3-7 images to your profile. Use all of them! Yes, you heard that right: *use all your picture slots, but more importantly, be very mindful of the pictures you upload.*

To ensure you use all your picture slots correctly, keep the following pro tips in mind:

Use 3-7 good photos

According to *Marni "personal wing girl" Kinrys*, a female dating coach for men, your dating profile should have three to five good profile pictures. As mentioned in the previous strategy, the primary profile picture should show your face. As Marni mentions, the remaining three slots should consist of a photograph that *shows you full-frame*, one that *shows you in a social setting but where you are still the center of attention*, and one that shows you *engaged in something you enjoy doing such as a hobby.*

Selfies are a no-no

Avoid having selfie shots or similar/related images. Data analyzed by Zoosk shows that having a selfie on your dating profile can lower your match and response rate by up to -8%.

Take it outdoors

Have at least one "outdoorsy" picture. The same data analyzed by Zoosk showed that having a full-body "outdoorsy" shot can increase your matches and message rate a staggering 203%.

Keep the pets out of the frame

Unless you are a vet and hell-bent on letting potential matches know you are one, keep your dog, cat, bird, and other pets out of the frame. According to the research analyzed by Zoosk, trying to impress women by posing with animals can decrease your matches and message response rates by up to 53%.

Kill it in Red

For a psychological advantage, make sure one of the pictures you upload to your dating profile shows you wearing the color red. According to various research studies, when you wear the color red, most women —and men— are likely to consider you more attractive compared to someone wearing any other color. Moreover, having a picture where you are wearing red —preferably the main profile picture— will help you stand out because after analyzing 12,000 photos, Tinder concluded that 72% of men had pictures where they were wearing neutral colors (56% for women).

Show off your left jaw

Have a portrait picture that shows the left side of your face and jaw —again, preferably the main profile picture. Research shows that people are fonder of left-side shots. This trick — called leftward bias— is why most famous portraits often show the left side of the subject's face. Scientists hypothesize that the left cheek (or the left side of the face) appears more expressive because we view it from the right half of the brain, the part involved with emotional responsiveness.

If you keep these tips in mind, you should be OK. Other important image-related tips you should keep in mind are:

Use "golden hour" photographs to your advantage

Data analyzed by OkCupid revealed that dating profiles that used photos taken shortly after sunrise or immediately before sunrise, called "the golden hour," appear more attractive. Researchers postulate that this effect is because the golden hue often present at these times enhances all other color-tones.

Dress to impress

Remember that a woman uses every photo you upload and have on your profile —including the setting and background— to make snap judgments about whether she would like to meet you and the kind of person she thinks you are. Because of this —a concept called thin-slicing— make sure that in all the photos you upload to your online dating profile, you appear well-dressed, or rather, a man who knows what he is doing with his clothes and life.

You do not have to be in a dark suit, white shirt, and tie in all of your pictures —even though data analyzed by PhotoFeeler indicates that a dark suit, light-colored shirt, and tie boosts competence. All you have to do is ensure that your pictures suggest that you are a man who cares about his physical appearance and who has a dress sense about what kind of clothes accentuate his physique.

Action shots never miss

Using action shots to your advantage is another psychological hack that will increase your attractiveness by a substantial percentage because it subconsciously tells women that you are an alpha male. An action shot shows you are a "man in control," something women love.

For instance, a picture where you seem engrossed in a fun, DIY project tells women that you are a man who likes to use his hands to build things, which will undoubtedly win you "dating points."

Keep in mind these photo tips as you choose which images to upload to your dating profile. Later on, we shall discuss various online dating profiles don'ts, and as we do, we will mention numerous photo mistakes you should avoid.

NOTE: You may have noted that we dedicated a fair amount of space to discussing the profile pictures you upload to your dating profile. The reason for this is because images are the first thing a woman will look at before she even thinks about looking at the rest of your online dating profile.

If your profile images stand out, especially if they do an excellent job of conveying your lifestyle and the kind of person you are, you have won as much as 80% of the online dating battle, and you can rest assured that you will have many matches and messages.

Since you now know what to do to optimize your profile photos and to make sure they are irresistible, we can move on and look at tips and strategies you can use to optimize other aspects of your online dating profile:

#: Show your description/bio some love

A collection of great images on your online dating profile is enough to get your foot in the door and to impress women into matching with you.

When your photos capture women's attention, the next place they will turn their consideration to is your profile description —or your bio, on some dating apps. You need to ensure that this aspect of your online dating profile is as awesome as your images and the rest of your dating profile.

As was the case with the previous strategies, here too, we shall discuss various tips you can use to ensure your dating profile has a compelling bio or description.

Before we do that, the most important thing you need to do to ensure that your online dating profile's bio or description "hooks and reels 'em in" is to *write it authentically.*

According to Marni Kinrys, your description should showcase your authentic self; it should not be pretentious or motivated by a desire to describe yourself as who you think women want you to be or the kind of person you think they would want to be with, when you are not that person.

Describe yourself as authentically as possible, yes, but at the same time, use the following hacks and tips to ensure that your description leaves women dying to know you and to become part of your life:

Be sincere and vulnerable

No matter what information you share on your dating profile, make sure you write it a way that conveys your sincerity and vulnerability.

The best way to create a sincere online dating description is to write it conversationally —as if you are talking to an old buddy. In this sense, conversationally means while you should utilize your words well —after all, most dating platforms limit the number of words you can use on your description— you should not be "sales-pitchy" or write the bio as if you are desperate to sell yourself. Write it a natural way that shows you know that another human being will be reading your profile and judging you by what you say.

When it comes to being vulnerable, the best way to create an online dating profile saturated with this sentiment is to open up about your quirkiness. If you are a goofball, let it shine in your description; if you like dancing in the rain, tell it —and perhaps show it using images. If you have a "weird fetish," do not be afraid to show it — but remember to keep it clean.

Being open about your quirkiness lets women know that you are comfortable with who you are and are confident and self-assured enough not to be afraid of being rejected or judged for being true to yourself.

Emotional availability is sexy

Spielmann et al. conducted a series of experiments to determine which of these two aspects of a profile online daters consider most important: *emotional availability* or *attractiveness*.

The social psychologists involved in the study concluded that given a choice between dating an attractive, emotionally unavailable person, and a less attractive but emotionally available person, most women —and men— go for the less attractive but emotionally available person.

Given that, the best way to use your dating profile bio to show you are emotionally available is to word your profile in a manner that illustrates your emotional maturity.

Focus on highlighting your people-centric hobbies such as festivals, camping, hiking, and the other things you do in a day or week that involve other people. When you show you are emotionally available, it will be easier to create connections that develop into meaningful relationships.

Follow the 70:30 Rule

Your bio should strike a balance between talking about yourself and talking about the traits you want in an ideal partner. According to a study conducted by Statistic Brain, an excellent way to balance this is to dedicate 70% of your bio to expressing who you are as a person, and 30% to describing the partner of your dreams— the core character traits and values you are looking for in a girlfriend. For instance, if you say you like festivals and camping, you can add that you are looking for someone with whom you can share these adventures.

Use the 4-sections strategy

Writing an attractive, attention-grabbing description is not always easy. In fact, balancing between saying too little, saying just enough, and saying too much can be a nerve-wracking undertaking.

To ease this anxiety, borrow the 4-sections strategy used by Vida Select. According to Vida, in addition to following the 70:30 rule, the best way to ensure your dating profile has an irresistible description is to segment the description into four sections.

- In the *first section*, use a *statement or headline that grabs attention*. Your attention grabber can be anything; it can be a quote, a pun, a smart play on words, etc. The general idea is to grab her attention. Vida notes that this part is a great way to introduce and describe some of your valuable character traits. It is also a great place to introduce some of the things you do.

- In the *second section, describe your job or something you pursue every day of your life.* Here, keep in mind that the idea is not to show how accomplished you are, but to illustrate the kind of life you live in a typical day or week. Vida recommends talking about some of the work-related activities you engage in every day.

- In the *third section*, you should *talk about your life outside of work and the exciting hobbies and interests you undertake every day*. Like the previous section, this section aims to give potential matches an idea of what it would be like to be your everyday girlfriend.

- In the *fourth section, describe your ideal partner.* Here, Vida notes that the essential thing to do is to cleverly outline the core attributes and values you consider most important in a mate —and to describe them in a conversational, exciting way.

Use these four words

PlentyofFish conducted a profile analysis that sought to determine which types of online dating descriptions were likelier to help men start committed relationships.

After examining more than 1.2 million profiles, they discovered that online dating profiles that had the words "romantic," "love," "relationship", and "old-fashioned" were most likely to lead to long-term relationships. Since you aim to use online dating to find a girlfriend and start a committed relationship, work these words into your profile description.

Use the magic of a conversational opener

It is easy to forget that while the aim behind your dating profile description is to give women an accurate idea of who you are and the kind of mate you want, its secondary objective is to help make starting a conversation stress-free.

Starting or ending your description with a conversational opener is a great way to give women ammo they can use to strike up a conversation once you match with them.

If you keep these tips in mind, you will create a great dating profile description that captures attention and "draws women in". In addition to these tips, make sure you also use humor, highlight what makes you a great catch —the qualities and character traits that make you worth knowing and going out with— and keep the description short, concise, and honest. And above all that, be genuine.

The pictures you add to your dating profile and the bio/description you create are the most critical aspects of your online dating profile. If you ace these two aspects, which you can do with a degree of ease now that you have the invaluable tips and strategies we have discussed, you will have no trouble attracting matches.

In addition to these primary strategies and tips, also keep the following in mind as you create your dating profile:

#: Your username matters too

On some dating platforms, you can use a username instead of your name. When that is the case, make sure your username stands out. A username that stands out is one that makes her curious about you.

The best way to do this is to avoid using a username that has numbers —LonelyHeart90— and to instead find a creative way to work your hobbies, interests, and attractive character traits into your username —SillyBilly, MountainMan, and BuiltToLast are all great examples.

If you want to go the strategic route, studies have shown that women find successful-sounding usernames more attractive and that they also have an open fondness for usernames that start with letters in the first part of the alphabet —A, B, C, etc. Starting your username with a letter in the first half of the alphabet is also advantageous because most dating sites adopt an "alphabetical Rolodex" system, which means when you use such a username, your profile will be among the first shown to women within your match criteria.

#: Reel them in with a catchy headline

On most online dating platforms and apps, adding a caption is an invaluable strategy because, in most instances, the headline is visible to "swipers."

The general rule here is to use a catchy, engaging, and enticing headline that draws attention. You can use your favorite quote; if you do not want to do that, word your headline to show you are authentic and confident.

If you would like help coming up with a catchy headline or generating ideas for quotes you can use on your dating profile, Vida Select has a mammoth list of dating profile headlines, while PairedList has an epic roster of dating profile quotes. Use them both to find inspiration, but remember to be genuinely and authentically you:

http://bit.ly/2EJ1XeS

http://bit.ly/35Qerxt

#: Consistency will get you far

Make sure that everything about your profile is consistent. If, for example, you say you like adventure, your profile pictures should highlight this aspect of your life. If you say you are a Netflix-and-chill kind of person, make sure everything about your profile reflects this sentiment.

Consistency is essential because if the notion of you a woman creates in her mind is not consistent with what you say you are, she will feel as if you are trying to deceive her into going out with you. For instance, if your username is, "AdventureSam" and your tagline/headline is "I am your next and last adventure," make sure everything about your profile screams, "I am nuts about adventures! Join me on my next adventure."

The more consistent you are, the easier it will be for women to create a clear image of the kind of person you are and the kind of lifestyle they would be getting themselves into if they decided to "give you a shot."

#: Keep it 100% honest

Can you remember what we said about being authentic? Well, this strategy cements that and relates to the strategy we just discussed.

After analyzing millions of profiles, Zoosk discovered that "honest" is the most used word when online daters are describing their ideal partner or match. Use all the description-creating strategies we have discussed thus far, yes, but more importantly, be authentic, honest, and open about who you are, what you want, and the kind of partner for which you are in the market.

#: Grammar and spelling matters

Bad spelling and grammar turn off high-quality women, the kind you want to attract and date. In fact, most women consider lousy grammar and spelling a pet peeve.

While your dating profile should not read like a Ph.D. thesis that you used a dictionary to write, you should at least spellcheck to make sure you catch typos and other grammatical mistakes. Writing, *"you could be hear with me"* instead of *"you could be here with me,"* will cost you valuable points. Showing you care about the image you portray online will win you bonus points with the kind of women you want to attract.

As mentioned at the start of this guidebook, the one thing that will ensure your success with online dating is the ability to take what you learn and implement it. Take the profile-creation strategies and tips we have discussed in this chapter and apply them, no matter how unconventional they seem at first. The results you achieve will make you immensely glad you did.

To close this chapter, we shall briefly look at three of the most common mistakes you should avoid when creating your online dating profile:

The 3 Most Lethal Dating Profile Mistakes Most Men Make (and How to Avoid Them)

Here are the most common —and most fatal— mistakes men make when creating their online dating profiles:

#1: Profile picture mistakes

Profile picture mistakes are the most common and the most lethal because, as we have mentioned earlier, women use the pictures you upload to your dating profile to determine if you are interesting, worth knowing, or worth dating.

Remember that women (and men, for that matter) "thin-slice" every aspect of every image you upload to your dating profile —including the background.

Since we have discussed the most crucial things you should do to ensure the images on your dating profile pop out and attract attention, here now are the profile-pictures mistakes you should avoid:

- **Do not use an old photo:** Instead, use your most recent, best photo —you can even seek professional help with this. Doing otherwise will be nothing short of setting yourself up for failure; after all, you will meet and date some of the women you match and talk with —is that not the plan? If you use an old photo, the women you meet for dates will feel deceived —and you may end up losing your chance to turn a great woman into a girlfriend.

- **Do not do pack your image slots with group shots:** Yes, have a photo showing you in a social setting, but make sure that even then, you are the center of attention. Where possible, make sure that such a picture is outdoorsy and shows you in action or pursuing something you love doing.

- **Do not do mirror selfies or ab shots:** No matter how "shredded" you are, or how fantastic a bathroom you have, under no circumstance should you upload a shirtless bathroom selfie or a picture of your abs —or your naked body for that matter. Additionally, you should avoid an all-selfies profile-picture line-up because it will make you look like a loner, narcissist, or self-centered bore of a person, and no woman wants to attach herself to that sort of man.

- **Do not filter your photos to death:** Remember that the general idea is to use your pictures to show women the kind of man you are, your interests, and the type of life you live, and to give them an idea of what they would be getting themselves into if they become your girlfriend. Over-filtering your photos goes against this purpose.

With pictures, the rule of thumb is to remember that the aim of the profile picture —and the other images you upload to your dating profile— is to arouse curiosity, invite, and then hook. Any photo that does not help you do this should not be part of your online dating profile.

#2: Description/bio mistakes

Again, your bio or description is the second thing women look at once the pictures on your profile captivate them. Make sure you follow the profile description/bio tips we discussed earlier, and while you do, avoid these mistakes:

- **Do not rant:** Do not use your description as a therapy session where you rant about specific feminine character traits you hate. Remember that the idea is to use your description to tell women about yourself and to use your profile pictures to show them the kind of man you are, what they can expect, and to explain the character traits you are looking for in a girlfriend.

- **Do not use words and phrases that instill a negative sentiment:** Your description should be conversational and positive. Avoid using any words that make you sound bitter, cynical, jaded, hostile, or negative. Remember that you should shoot for warm and inviting.

- **Do not say how terrible you are at self-description:** Saying things like I'm not very good at describing myself is a big mistake you should avoid. If you cannot express who you are in 500 words or less, why in God's name would a woman want to be with you, a man who does not know himself? You want to show you know, value, and hold yourself in high esteem —which is why you have taken the time to describe who you are, your lifestyle, and the kind of girlfriend you are ready to welcome into your life.

- **Do not be vulgar:** There is nothing wrong with adding one or two swear-words into your description. However, being excessively rude or using a ton of swear-words turns women off. If you must optimize your dating profile with a swear word, ensure that the sentiment communicated is your passion/enthusiasm for something. Anything less will be akin to shooting yourself in the foot.

- **Do not overuse emojis:** Emojis have their place on your dating bio; in fact, emojis are a great way to give women an idea of what you are about and what you like without using too many words, but overusing them tells women you are an ineffective communicator.

When crafting a bio for your online dating profile, the most important thing you want to keep in mind is authenticity: create your description in a way that shows women what you are about, what they should expect, and tell them why they should be itching to become your girlfriend and "a fixture" in your life.

#3: Congruency mistakes

Congruency mistakes are some of the most commonly committed by male online daters.

Remember that what when what you say —your bio or description— and what you show —your photos— lacks consistency, it will give women cause for pause and make you appear doggy. No woman wants to date an inconsistent man. Avoid this mistake by making sure your profile communicates a consistent message and that you "show instead of tell."

If you implement the various strategies, hacks, and tips we have discussed in this chapter of the guide, you will create a compelling online dating presence that will attract matches and have women itching to get to know you better.

Action Step

This section of the guide has covered a ton of actionable dating strategies you can use to your advantage. Utilize them because, as repeatedly stated throughout this guide, your success with online dating hinges on your willingness to apply what you learn.

Now that you have chosen a dating app, created a dating profile, and optimized it, your profile will be a match-generating machine. The next step of the process is to engage your matches by starting stimulating conversations. You also need to drive those conversations towards building attraction, rapport, chemistry, and a date.

The chapters in the next section of the guide show you how to do this like a pro.

Section 2

Priming your Matches, Building Attraction, Flirting, Pre-Dating, & Working Towards a Date

Welcome to the second section of this guidebook.

This section will equip you with the essential steps, strategies, and tips you need to have —and to use— to build attraction with your matches as you flirt and work towards dates, searching for the girlfriend of your dreams.

Among several other things, this section will cover areas such as:

- *How to open conversations with your matches in a way that helps you stand out without appearing creepy, and that builds immediate rapport and mutual attraction.*

- *How to master the language of flirtation, and more importantly, how to use flirtation in a way that builds sexual chemistry and that has your matches itching to meet you for coffee, drinks, lunch, or dinner— and start something special.*

- *The pre-dating process, its importance, how to navigate through it, how long it should last, and how to turn the interest and attraction created during this stage into an actual date or relationship.*

- *The dating signs you should look out for as you seek to determine if you have met or found the right partner.*

- *How to avoid dating misunderstandings, coming off as an online dating creep, and other common but costly mistakes that most men commit.*

- *The various dos and don'ts you should pay close attention to when working towards turning your match into an offline date and a potential long-term girlfriend.*

And so much, much more.

After reading the various chapters that make up this section of the guidebook, you will know how to start conversations with your online matches, drive these conversations towards building sexual chemistry, and turning a "swipe-left" into a date.

The first thing we shall discuss is how to start conversations with your match(es) online in a manner that helps you stand out from a sea of other men pining for her attention.

Chapter 4: Five Strategies to Help You Master the Art of Sending First Messages That Get Responses

If you implemented the various strategies and tips that saturated the third chapter of this guidebook —the section on how to create an irresistible online dating profile— your dating profile should be a non-stop match-generating machine.

While this is amazing and is the first step to using online dating like a pro, you cannot stop there if you are deeply committed to using this avenue to find a remarkable long-term girlfriend.

Once your phone chimes with notification after notification of match after match, you need to start conversations with your matches, and you need to do so in an intelligent, fun way that helps you stand out.

Unfortunately, starting conversations with strangers is often an anxiety-inducing process, more so when the stranger in question is a beautiful woman with whom you would like to create a meaningful connection that can lead to her being your girlfriend.

This chapter aims to provide you with first-message strategies guaranteed to help you spark off attention-grabbing conversations with women online, and do so in a way that, in addition to helping you stand out, helps create rapport, a meaningful connection, attraction, and moving towards a date.

As Carson Kressley points out, sometimes the best way to learn is to *"jump off the deep end and learn to swim."*

Let's jump off the deep end:

#1: First, put on your spy glasses

After matching with a woman, do not be in a rush to say hello or to open up the communication channel —no matter how excited you are that a woman you had hoped would "swipe left" on you actually did.

The effectiveness of your first message, and more importantly, whether your first message stands out enough to capture her interest and warrant a response will largely depend on your *genuineness*. You cannot be genuine if you do not take the time to tailor your message to the specific woman you want to reach out to because you want to get to know her.

Even if you swiped left on her because her profile screamed, *"she is the one,"* do not send that first message without looking over her profile again —even better, do it more than once.

As you do this fair bit of "spying on her," keep in mind that the general idea is not to be an internet creep. The purpose is to "feel her out" and mark the noticeable things about her and her profile that you can use to open a personalized conversation.

#2: "Hi" doesn't cut it

Yes, after "spying" on her, the first thing you have to do is greet her; that is an inescapable fact. However, if you go with a standard "Hi," "Hello," "Hey," or any other similarly bland, vanilla greeting, the chances are high that she will downright ignore your message altogether.

Your salutation is vital because how you word it will have an impact on the impression of you that she creates in her mind. Keep in mind that the idea is to catch her attention well enough for her to want to read the message that follows the salutation. If you open with "Hi," which is what 23% of men do, you are setting yourself up to fail.

If "Hi" and other such variants do not cut it, what *should* you do, you ask? Well, you can use the better salutations: "How's it going?", "How you doin'?", "What's up?", and any other such open-ended question. When you do, your chances of drawing a reply are higher than those of the man who uses "hellos."

According to the data crunchers over at OkCupid, using a non-traditional salutation/opener increases the chances of a reply by as much as 27%.

When thinking about which opener to use, the primary thing to keep in mind is that you should give her something with which to work. For instance, when you open with "How's it going?", you give her some material she can use to continue talking to you —she may decide to speak with you about her day, her life, work, etc.

#3: Attentiveness will get you far

Ok, now you know what to type into that message box first: *a non-conventional greeting/salutation*. If you stop there, or if you send nothing but that non-traditional hello, you may get a response, yes, but you may also not get one —just greeting her and stopping there will make you seem lazy and somewhat disinterested in her.

To guarantee that she responds to your message, couple the salutation with a more substantive message. Your best bet here is to follow your greeting with a message that references something on her profile, which is why the first strategy we mentioned here is to "spy" on her profile so that you can have some ammunition.

For instance, if she says she likes tattoos and you noticed something about her wrist tattoo, reference it and then ask her a question —questions are a golden strategy that will get her talking to you because as humans, we love talking about ourselves and, therefore, when you give her a chance to speak with you, she will take it.

Again, after analyzing millions of messages, the data crunchers over at OkCupid concluded that messages that use phrases such as "you mention…" or "I noticed…", showing her you paid attention to her profile and are now curious about her interests, increase the chances of a reply by 40-50%

Here, the rule of thumb is to follow your greeting with a message that refers to her interests, or in a case where you have mutual interests, to mention these interests —it helps you work towards creating a conversation that helps build meaningful connections.

Use the spy work you put into checking out her profile to determine which message to attach to the greeting. Also, and this is somewhat important, attach a question to your message. It will show her your genuine desire to get to know her and give her a reason to keep talking to you.

#4: You can "novel" your way into her "block list"

Now that you know what to do to write your match (es) the first message, and what to write to increase your chances of getting a reply, you may feel tempted to think that, *"mention a mutual interest —or one of her interests— and then ask her a related question"* means you should write her a novel. If you thought that, then you would be wrong.

In addition to being overwhelming, using her inbox as your "brain-dump notebook" is likely to turn her off because, let's face it, the high-quality girlfriend you want to attract is probably busy "getting it" and does not have a whole lot of time to read long paragraphs.

Moreover, when you go overboard and write an overly long initial message, she is likely to think you are an odd duck, trying too hard, or assuming too much about her —being too familiar—, and the more probable your chances her seeing you as coming on too strong.

A good rule of thumb is to keep it under 20 words. When you keep it short, simple, and easy to read, it makes your message easier to digest and understand, which makes the chances of a reply higher.

NOTE: It is imperative to mention here that the goal of the first message is to open a conversation that builds rapport. The simpler you keep it, the better. However, once you open communication and are talking and "vibing", there is nothing wrong with writing your dream girl longer messages. Matter of fact, once she shows a keen interest in you —which is what replying to your compelling messages and questions is— you can keep her interested in you by sharing more about yourself and giving her a chance to do the same.

Importantly, even when you have a few messages between you and some rapport building —rapport means a back and forth, enjoyable communication channel— do not overshare or write her overly long messages if she is not doing the same. Prime her into liking you more by mirroring her. If she writes you 10-word sentences, do the same. If she uses certain words, do the same.

Now that we are talking about rapport, priming, and keeping her interested, you also need to:

#5: Keep it light, fun, flirty, and ongoing

In the initial contact —the first few messages— keep the messages light, fun, and flirty (more about flirting in a second).

Here is the thing:

Whenever you are doing something or meeting new people, there is always an air of excitement; you want your initial online conversation with women online to follow the same principle. You want to make talking to you to feel thrilling and new so much so that she looks forward to opening her inbox and seeing a message from you. The best way to do this is to keep your messages light, fun, and flirty.

Share interesting things about yourself and lead her into sharing interesting things about herself —that way, you will build a palpable rapport and may end up chatting long into the night, especially when your time being online coincides with hers.

If you guessed that keeping it light, fun, and flirty means you should avoid some topics, you are right.

The first thing you want to avoid is being overly complimentary, especially in the first several messages. Yes, it is OK to give a girl you like a compliment, but even then, hold it until you have built some rapport or, if you have to compliment her in the first few messages, drop it in casually and make it very specific to her interests, not her physical attributes.

On physical-related compliments, data analyzed by OkCupid showed that 31% of men compliment women by saying things like she is "hot, "cute," "beautiful," or "sexy."

Since you want to drive the conversation towards a long-term commitment, you should not give her physical-related compliments —at least not at first— because mentioning her physical attributes will give her the wrong impression about your interest in her.

As an example of what kind of compliments to give, you could say, *"I like your style; I too could live in jeans and a T-shirt. Are you a Levi or Wrangler kind of girl?"* Such a statement compliments her about her style —not how "good her ass looks in them jeans"— and lets her know you have a common interest, and then asks her a question. You cannot go wrong with such compliments and related statements.

To keep your initial conversation, light, fun, exciting, and flirty, the other thing you want to avoid is heavy, emotion-laden topics. Her inbox is not the place or the time to "get to know" her religious and political beliefs or to talk about sex —especially keep away from sex-related conversations online.

The keyword you should keep in mind here is *playful*; the more playful, light and fun you are, the easier it will be to get her to talk and flirt with you, keep her interested, and keep the conversation moving towards setting a date.

Since we are talking about being playful and lighthearted, flirting is one of the best means through which to do this.

In the next chapter, we shall discuss 25 flirtatious phrases you should use with your matches during the pre-date phase of the online dating process.

Chapter 5: The Language of Flirting: 25 Phrases Women Love

From the moment you start talking to her online to the moment you set a meet-up, you want to build excitement, chemistry, and attraction so that she is eager to go out with you. Flirting, when done the right way, is the best way to do this.

Since you already know what to say —and not say— in the messages you send her, this chapter will equip you with a couple of dozen flirtatious phrases women love and that you should utilize where doing so feels natural:

#1:

"I would love to …"

You can finish this statement in several ways. For instance, you could say, *"I would love to know what you think about topic X,"* or *"Phone conversations are so underrated nowadays. I would love to hear your voice."*

Irrespective of how you finish the statement, it works well because it communicates your genuine interest in her and is also a prompting phrase that will have her opening up and talking to you.

#2:

"I know ..."

Like the previous statement, you can complete the ellipsis in various flirtatious ways. For instance, you could say, *"Your bio says you love warm hugs, so, I'm sending you a warm hug to comfort you after a long day at work,"* or *"I know you are a big Star Wars fan. I have two tickets to ''Star Wars: The Rise of Skywalker''. Join me?"*

In both instances, you are letting her you want to connect with her, communicating your interest, showing her you care, and in the last statement, asking her out in a way she is unlikely to refuse, especially if she is a true Star Wars fan. Moreover, this is another prompting statement you can use to drive a conversation that builds rapport and attraction.

#3:

"How can I ..."

"How can I brighten your evening?", "How can I bring a smile to your face?", "How can I win your heart?", or even *"How can I help?"* are great examples of how you can use this prompting statement to flirt with her.

The statement works because it shows you care and are an emotionally intelligent man, as only an emotionally intelligent man would show concern for a woman he has not met.

#4:

"By the way, I'm still wearing the smile you gave me when we first talked."

Nonchalantly referring to how she makes you feel (such as when you first spoke or met online) will make her feel good about the impact she has on you. Don't hesitate to let her know!

#5:

"Are you on ...?"

Again, you can finish this in many ways. For instance, *"Are you on Facebook?"* lets her know that you would like to connect outside the dating site, which helps build chemistry and rapport because it shows you want the budding relationship to progress further.

#6:

"Do you use ..."

Here are two contrasting examples: *"Do you use Cleopatra's beauty regimen? Your smile is just too breathtaking and your face too radiant",* or, *"Do you use social media?"* The first message is smack-you-in-the-face flirtatious. It tells her that you have noticed her beautiful smile and face, which will make her feel nice. The second statement is subtler. It lets her know that your interest in her has progressed deeper, which will also stir up pleasant feelings in her.

#7:

"Our online conversations brighten up my evenings. I can't wait for the day I get to stare into your eyes as we chat the night away."

Casually mentioning how much you enjoy chatting with her will stir up her feel-good hormones. Saying how you cannot wait for the day when you are comfortable enough to stare into each other's eyes as you chat the night away will let her know that you want to create a meaningful relationship.

#8:

"Talking with you has been on my mind all day."

Nonchalantly mentioning how she has been on your mind will communicate how interested and attracted to her you are, which will leave her feeling wanted and valued.

#9:

"Has anybody ever told you ..."

Being another prompting phrase, you can use this statement flirtatiously in various ways. For instance, you could say, *"Has anyone ever told you that your smile could give rainbows a run for their money?"*, or, *"Has anyone ever told you how amazing you look in red?"*

Both statements will leave her feeling amazing; they will also communicate your sincere interest in her.

#10:

"There's nothing I want more right now than to be with you."

You are letting her know that you have thought about being with her—you are priming her for the probability of being *"your person"*—and that after thinking about it, there's nothing you would want more right now. Such a statement is likely to leave her feeling "all-gooey for you inside".

#11:

"Your ___."

It could be, *"Your smile drives me crazy,"* or *"Your witty banter is something I look forward to every day."* Either way, using this statement lets her know how amazing you think she is.

#12

"Do you know what I love the most about you?"

Revealing that you love something about her is a great way to flirt, stir up attraction, build rapport, and keep the conversation going.

#13:

"Tell me about your most meaningful experience."

At first glance, this statement does not sound flirtatious. It is, because it shows you like her enough to want to know about the deep things that make her who she is, and, secondly, because wanting to know about the things that move her helps create intimacy.

#14:

"Every time my dating app sends me a notification, I open it hoping it's from you."

Letting her know how much you look forward to hearing from her will leave her wanting to talk to you more because she knows you appreciate it.

#15:

"How you doin'?"

In addition to telling her that you are somewhat fun and have a degree of care about what she is up to, this message has an undertone: you are also asking because you would not mind joining her in doin' whatever she's doin'. "How you doin'?" is also a leading statement that can lead to all sorts of flirtatious conversations.

#16:

"What's your To-do list like, and how can I get on it?"

The first thing this message does is to let her know that you can be silly and fun, and women like men who can make them laugh and who do not take themselves too seriously.

Secondly, it lets her know that you want to become an integral part of her daily life (the "To-do list" reference), which gives her the impression that you want to create a meaningful connection.

#17:

"You were in my dreams last night."

"You were in my dreams last night" is a splendid way to let her know how much she excites you, which is likely to stimulate her even more and to open up the conversation to further flirting. A typical reply to this message is, *"Oh? Tell me what you dreamt about."*

#18:

"Let's play a coin toss game. Heads we do something you love this weekend. Tails I buy you dinner Friday night."

First, you let her know that you have a fun streak. Secondly, the statement tells her that you are eager to meet her, which will help bump up the attraction-stakes.

#19:

"How does drinks tomorrow night sound?"

Leading statements and questions such as this one let a woman know that you are ready to take the plunge, meet her, and have a one-on-one conversation —in other words, to take the relationship offline.

#20:

"Since we both like to eat, I don't see why we can't eat X [a meal you both like] together."

This message is about taking things offline and moving the relationship forward, which is excellent because texting has limitations when it comes to knowing someone and cultivating a deep, meaningful connection.

#21:

"What's your most fun weekend activity, and when can we do it?"

When you ask her about her interests and then show her that you are open to engaging in them with her, you become someone she can see herself spending time with, which is a win for you. Adding *"when can we do it"* is a covert way of telling her you would like to spend time with her off the dating app.

#22:

"Tell me about your dream first-date."

Casually letting her know that you are thinking about "her first date" is enough to communicate that you want to have one with her and to do it in a way that fulfills some of her first-date dreams/fantasies.

To add some hot sauce to the message, you can add, *"and the best time to pick you up for it."* Adding this lets her know that you want to be part of her fulfilled dreams/fantasies, which lets her know you are looking to create a meaningful partnership.

#23:

"If you say yes to ___ [dinner, watching a movie together, going out for drinks, etc.], I'll let you hold my hand."

In addition to being fun and sassy, such a message stirs her into thinking about what it would be like to be together out in public, holding hands as boyfriend and girlfriend.

#24:

"I can see myself falling for you."

Telling her how you can see yourself falling in love with her gets her to think about how it would be to be in love and/or in a relationship with you, which is a good thing because it lets her know you are serious about turning what you have going on between you into something substantive.

#25:

"Thinking about how great it will be to sit across from you (tomorrow night) makes me as giddy as a schoolboy."

Nonchalantly mentioning how excited you are to meet up with her excites her about the prospect just as much as it does you.

If you use these 25 flirtatious phrases and statements, you should be able to keep your conversation with her playful, fun, and moving towards a date.

NOTE: With some of these phrases, you should not be afraid to use emojis to your advantage. According to AJ Harbinger, a relationship coach and the founder of ArtofCharm, adding emojis to flirty messages accentuates the spirit of playfulness, which can make the conversation exciting and keep it moving towards a date.

The best time to use these statements is during the pre-date phase of dating. The next chapter will give you more information about pre-dating and how to navigate through it like the Michael Jordan of Dating.

Chapter 6: Everything You Need to Know about Pre-dating

Pre-dating is modern verbiage that can mean one of two things:

> *a)   The phase of online dating between the first message sent between a "matched pair" and the first date.*
>
> *b)   A casual date before the "main" or "actual" date*

In both instances, pre-dating is a good thing.

In the first instance, it gives you a chance to connect with your match(es) on a deeper level beyond the online dating bio, and in the second instance, a casual pre-date (we can call it a "short date") is a great way to do away with some of the anxiety generally attached to the first date.

In this chapter, we are going to discuss both scenarios.

#: The Pre-dating phase

Pre-dating is a relatively new concept and stage of dating. Researchers **postulate that it started in 2010.**

When we use the term pre-dating to refer to the phase between when you send a woman the first message to the moment you meet-up for a date, the purpose of the process is to "feel each other out," and to determine if you have a "connection" before committing to a first date or to "seeing each other."

From this perspective, while the name sounds fancy, pre-dating is just messaging back and forth, flirting, and building rapport and attraction as you work towards setting up a meet-up or date.

When we look at pre-dating from this perspective, a question you are likely to have is "How long to pre-date?"

What's the ideal duration of the pre-date phase?

There is no right or wrong answer.

Since the pre-dating phase purposes to help you "get to know each other" and to "feel each other out", it can last as long as it lasts.

However, and this is fundamentally important, online dating conversations have a way of fading out when all you do is talk, talk, and then talk some more without ever taking the plunge and asking her out for a meet-up.

As such, you do not want to "just talk" to her. You want to ensure that every conversation you have with her is working towards a date. Matter of fact, to enhance your chance of meeting and dating as many women as possible, and out of those dates, meeting the girlfriend of your dreams and then committing to her, ask your match(es) out after a few instances of back and forth messages. Five messages both ways should be enough.

To help you figure out the ideal length of the pre-dating phase, keep this in mind:

> 1. *Start stimulating conversations with your match(es)*
>
> 2. *Drive the conversations forward by being fun, light, and flirtatious, and then,*
>
> 3. *After she sends you five messages, casually invite her out for drinks, coffee, dinner, a movie, or whatever, perhaps something fun you would both enjoy.*

With these simple three steps in mind, you can rest assured that your pre-date phase will not be so overly long that it leads to a dull, dying conversation.

Advantages of the pre-date phase

The first advantage of the pre-dating period is that it gives you a chance to check each other out and determine whether you have anything in common —or can have a stimulating conversation, which is how you build a meaningful connection.

Bantering before planning a date gives you a chance to create trust and e-chemistry (electronic chemistry). The possibilities are high that if you have e-chemistry, you will have offline chemistry as well. At any rate, if you have e-chemistry and it builds up to a meet-up, even if the meet-up does not pan out well and you do not end up meeting the woman of your dreams, you will have had a good conversation with a great woman.

#: Pre-dating

A pre-date, which is *a low-key, zero-pressure, no-strings-attached meet-up between two people who have chatted online but have never met offline,* is a great way to ease into dating without feeling anxious.

Pre-dating essentials

A fundamental thing you need to understand about a pre-date is that is has nothing to do with being a low-key way to have sex with a woman before you take her out on an actual date. That pre-dating is a way to get **"free sex without spending a dime on a woman" is a misconception**, one you should not buy into or believe.

A pre-date is as the name suggests: a date before a date (a pre-date). It is a no-expectations meet-up between two people who are interested in each other enough to want to break the anxiety of "a major date with a beautiful woman or handsome man" by going on a low-key "short date".

Now that you know that, here are the essentials you should keep in mind when planning a pre-date:

Step 1

First, how you suggest or bring up the pre-date is very fundamental. While you can ask your Tinder match to *"go out on a pre-date with you,"* you want to be coyer with it lest she assumes you want to "hook-up" without taking her to dinner first, which is a possibility because online dating has jaded women.

You should bring up the pre-date in a cute and fun way. For instance, you could tell her, *"You're such a witty banterer. I can't wait to spend time with you offline. Since I get very nervous on first dates, help me out by spending two hours of your Wednesday evening after work with me getting some coffee/drinks."*

It is probable that she gets nervous on first dates, too, and would be open to a low-key, short, no-expectations meet-up when proposed in the manner mentioned above.

Step 2

A pre-date aims to slice away at some of the anxiety and awkwardness of a first date. Therefore, you should keep the pre-date short.

Tammy Greene, a Licensed Mental Health Counselor, suggests keeping the pre-date below an hour long. You are free to use your judgment, but make sure you keep the date as short as comfortable; otherwise, it becomes a date-date, which is counterintuitive and adds to the pressure.

Meet-up for something non-committal —not as committal as a formal date— such as a walk at the local park, some street food, ice cream, or even coffee. Keep the pre-date budget to $5 or below per person.

Step 3

Do not schedule the pre-date to coincide with weekends or any other recreational time. It should preferably be on a workday, so that should either of you flake out, it does not throw your "recreational plans" into a tailspin.

Step 4

Keep the pre-date a bantering affair, which means you should avoid "heavy" topics. Instead, keep the conversation light, and after spending an hour or two with each other, avoid the awkward pressure of having to talk about whether you will go on a follow-up date by ending the date with a pleasant, "It was nice to meet you" and going on your merry way. Then, after reviewing the meeting, reach out via phone and make follow-up plans for the first date (if the pre-date was successful. If not, you can always say, *"You are great, but ..."*).

NOTE: It is <u>VERY</u>, <u>VERY</u>, <u>VERY</u> important that if you are going to do a pre-date, you and the woman in question be on the same page about nature, purpose, and rules of the pre-date. Open communication is your friend here.

Keep in mind that the goal of this date is to familiarize yourself with each other and, in so doing, decide if you would like to see each other more and then slice away some of the tension, anxiety, and awkwardness of going all-out on a first date.

As long as you are open about your intentions, very few women will be uneasy with the idea of going on a short date that helps you both decide if you have a connection worth exploring further.

Chapter 7: The Creep Factor; How to Avoid Being Misunderstood & Other Mistakes

Webster's Online Dictionary defines a creep {noun} as *"an unpleasant or obnoxious person."*

As you navigate through your online dating journey, how you approach women will be the thing that determines whether you come off as a creep —and get "ghosted," reported, or blocked altogether— or as an authentic man who is worth dating.

Since how you approach women online is what will determine the nouns and adjectives these women use to describe you, to avoid coming off as a dating creep, all you have to do is to apply to your advantage everything you have learned from the second section of this book.

To recap, you can <u>avoid being categorized as a creep</u> by optimizing your online dating profile —including your pictures and bio— the right way. From there, you need to follow the tips on how to send the first message and to use messaging in a way that builds rapport and flirtation, and that drives the interaction towards a pre-date or actual date.

If you follow that advice, you should have no cause for worry because you will be communicating with the women you meet online from a position of genuine interest and a desire to get to know them, which is how you come off as an authentic man instead of an internet creep.

This chapter aims to add to what you have already learned about how to start genuine online interactions by outlining the various things you should avoid doing to ensure the women you meet online do not label you a creep.

How to Avoid The "Creep" Label

Here is how to avoid coming off as a creep:

#: Keep it PG13

When discussing how to craft an irresistible online dating profile, one of the strategies we discussed was the need to keep your profile clean by avoiding sexy bathroom shots or pictures of your naked body —or junk, for that matter. You should follow that advice and extend it to all areas of your interactions.

Keeping it PG13 means not sending her "dick pictures", and all forms of unsolicited images for that matter; unless she asks for a photo, do not send her one. The only exception here is funny memes and GIFs, and even then, you should keep them clean, especially if you are yet to establish a palpable attraction with the woman in question.

Now that we are talking about keeping it PG13:

#: Keep off the sex talk

In your first ten conversations with a woman you just met online, DO NOT even think about mentioning the word sex. Yes, sex is important to you; it is important to her too. However, like physical-based compliments —the next strategy— mentioning sex in your first few interactions sets off alarms in her mind and without meaning to, she will think you are a sex pervert who is looking for an "easy lay."

Additionally, given that you are reading this book, you are in the market for a long-term companion (a girlfriend). Since that is the case, you have to know that the high-quality, beautiful woman you want probably gets unsolicited sex offers from men all the time. Mentioning sex will give her no choice but to bundle you with the men she intends to filter out, ignore, or block, which is definitely something you do not want to happen.

#: Keep physical-based compliments to yourself

Although mentioned at another part of this guide, because of its importance, it is worth repeating: the first few messages you send a match, but especially the first message, should have no mention of her body.

Only compliment her body after building attraction and flirtation, and even then, word it correctly —you can use some of the flirting phrases we discussed in chapter 5.

#: Serial texting

When you match with a woman you really like, it is easy to go overboard by serial-texting her, especially when she takes a while to respond or does not respond as fast as you would want.

Serial-texting is a common mistake; if you commit it, rest assured that she will label you an online dating creep and un-match you before even thinking about reading your chains of text messages.

Again, remember that the high-quality woman you want to attract is probably busy living her life and "getting hers". Respect that —and her, too— by showing some restraint.

Do not send her more than two messages at a go without waiting for a reply; even then, approach the two-messages strategy with a bit of caution. The best plan is to go text-for-text. When you message her, wait for her reply and then send yours. Only send a second follow-up message if she takes as long as, say, a week to reply, and keep the follow-up light, not sounding anxious or needy.

#: Over-forwardness

Flirting with her will help build rapport and attraction, yes, but even then, it is fundamentally, <u>FUNDAMENTALLY</u> vital that you bide your time before moving the conversation in that direction.

In a world where women have grown accustomed to hearing things like "hey cutie, hottie, babe, etc." or statements such as "you have a bangin' body," jumping into flirtation too fast, especially when you are still strangers whose paths just crossed, will trip her creep-radar and get you unmatched or blocked.

Above all this, keep in mind that when you match with a woman, the best way to avoid coming off like an internet creep is to remember that at the other end of the message box is an intelligent, beautiful woman who, like you, can judge you based on what you say. Make sure you say things that make her want to talk to you and that show her you can be her dream partner.

If you do this and remember to be authentic and genuinely interested in establishing a connection with the woman you match with, you should have no problems with avoiding the creep tag.

To ensure women on dating platforms do not misunderstand you or label you creepy, you also need to avoid costly dating-profile mistakes.

Let us briefly talk about how to avoid such mistakes:

Dating Profile Phrases You Should Not Use

In chapter three, we talked about three of the most lethal dating-profile mistakes most men make and how to avoid them.

This section adds to that by discussing specific phrases you should omit from your dating profile —unless you want women to misunderstand you or your intentions.

#: "Whatever else you want to know, ask."

The first thing you need to know about this phrase is that women see it on men's dating profiles all the time.

Secondly, the statement negates the very purpose of having an online dating bio in the first place: *to get to know each other.* Using it makes you look shady, like someone who has something to hide or is too lazy to give potential partners enough information to spark a conversation.

#: "I recently came out of a relationship."

Unless the idea you want to communicate is that you are looking for a rebound relationship, keep this phrase out of your bio; no woman wants to be a rebound partner.

Worse, adding this statement to your bio tells potential mates that you are not over the ended relationship and that you are, therefore, not emotionally available or stable enough to start something new.

Before you use this phrase, remember that the best way to craft a fantastic dating profile is to dedicate 70% of the space to outlining your outstanding character traits, interests, values, etc., and 30% to describing the character traits and ideals of the woman you want to meet and welcome into your life.

#: "I love …"

Phrases such as *"I love walking in the rain," "I love drinking a glass of wine under the moonlight,"* and the cringe-worthy, *"I love traveling and long walks on the beach"* are all clichés that should not appear anywhere on the precious piece of real estate that is your dating-profile bio.

Such phrases reveal very little about you —most people love the beach and traveling— and they, therefore, contraindicate the purpose of your bio, which is to let potential mates know who you are, your interests, values, and what drives you.

Avoid all cliché phrases by going into the specifics of why you love certain things. For instance, instead of saying how much you love the beach, communicate what it makes you feel.

You can say something like, *"Nothing is as awe-inspiring as watching the sunset over the waters of an ocean whose shores I have never been on before".* Such a statement communicates that you love to travel as well as what you love the most about being at the beach.

#: "I expect you to be …"

This phrase can also appear as, *"I want a partner who is loving, kind, hardworking, etc."* Here is the thing: "blah, blah, blah" is what she will think as she read this.

There is nothing wrong with using your bio to write about the character traits and values you are looking for in a partner. However, using a "shopping list" of attributes you want to find in a partner will give the impression that you are looking for the *perfect* partner and are uncompromising about it, which will cost you valuable points since no one is perfect and tagging your expectations on potential partners will intimidate them into swiping right.

3 Additional Online Dating Mistakes You Should Avoid

In addition to profile-dating mistakes, also avoid the following mistakes:

#: Vague language and generality

Using words such as "fun-loving, honest, smart," and other such phrases does very little to communicate who you are or what makes you tick. Do not make this mistake.

Instead, keep in mind that your purpose —especially when it comes to crafting your bio and description— is to give women an idea of the values and character traits that make you attractive, or that attract you to a partner.

#: Using the wrong profile pictures

Various sections of this guidebook —including the segment on how to create an irresistible online-dating profile— have talked deeply about the need to use good profile images.

The most common mistakes here are using unflattering pictures, failing to use your profile pictures to show women your lifestyle, and not using all your photograph slots.

#: Not messaging enough and messaging too much before setting up a date

Remember that once you match with a girl, the only way to get to know her and to build attraction is to message her. Do so!

At the same time, remember that online conversations tend to putter out when talk, talk, and talk some more is all you do. You want to establish a cordial back-and-forth, playful dialog with her so that by the time you are sending each other the fifth-to-tenth message, you are comfortable enough with each other to ask her out casually.

Since you now know which mistakes to avoid to ensure that women do not misunderstand you, let's move on to the next chapter where we shall talk about what to do —and not do— to score a date.

Chapter 8: Scoring a Date: Dos and Don'ts

At this point in the guide, you have everything you need to move your online conversations with women towards a date. You know how to start first messages, how to avoid coming off as a creep, how to message women in a manner that builds rapport and attraction, and how to flirt with women online until they are itching to go out with you.

This chapter will continue equipping you with invaluable strategies you can use to turn your matches and conversations with the women you meet online into in-person meetings by giving you a list of things you should and should not do to score a date.

The Dos

As you work towards scoring and setting a date with her, remember to:

Be open-minded

As you navigate through online dating, remember to keep an open mind because not every woman you meet will be the perfect match, and not every conversation you start will lead to a date.

Being open-minded will also allow you to respect other people's opinions, needs, and desires, which is especially important in the online dating space where people go into the venture with different expectations.

Use the right app for your dating needs

While this is not precisely "date-related", it is a crucial thing to keep in mind because of the broad scope of dating platforms and apps.

Since you desire a girlfriend, make sure you are using the right dating app —we talked about how to make sure of this— because different dating platforms serve different relationship needs. If you are using a "hook-up based" dating platform expecting to snag a date that leads to a long-term relationship, you will be setting yourself up for failure.

Stick to a moral code

No matter how tempting it is to exaggerate aspects of your dating profile to make yourself look like a great catch, do not give in to the temptation because, eventually, you will have to meet these women.

If you lie about things such as your physical attributes, even if you use "fake" profile pictures, women will sniff you out —Google Images to the rescue— and once they realize you are fake, you can rest assured that you will have no dates.

Ask questions

Questions are a great way to keep the conversation stimulating and ongoing; plus, the more you talk with her, the easier it is to build rapport and attraction, to flirt, and to direct the conversation towards a date.

Be authentic and genuine

Be yourself! If you are weird, quirky, charming, or funny, be that person. Being yourself creates a solid foundation for curiosity, trust, and communication, all of which can help you work your way to asking her out.

Moreover, your opinions, interests, and hobbies are the things that drive you. Being true to the person you are will help you share openly with the women you interact with, which will make finding the right partner more probable, which will increase the chances of her saying yes when you ask her out on a date.

Take it all in stride

While it may be feminine-directed, the saying, "you may have to kiss a thousand frogs before you find prince charming —or "princess charming in this case—" applies to online dating more than it does anywhere else.

Remember that you may have to talk to hundreds of women before you close a date or find a good match. Be ready for that. Be prepared for rejection, "ghosting," rude women, and all manner of crazies. Take it all in stride and no matter what happens, do not feel disheartened.

Treat online dating as a fun adventure and have fun with it. If you stick with it and keep implementing the various tips and strategies we have discussed in this guide, you will come out on top.

The Don'ts

The things to avoid as you work towards a date include:

Do not be a stalker

Being curious about your match is perfectly normal. However, stalking her on social media, especially when she has not shared her social media handles with you, will quickly get you labeled an internet creep.

No matter how curious you are, let the rapport, trust, and attraction build up until your matches feel comfortable enough to share such private information with you.

Do not play mind games

Online dating is not tic tac toe or chess. Avoid playing mind games because, newsflash, no one wins such games. When you match with women you do not feel intimately connected to, man up and say it; do not drag out the relationship hoping that it will turn into something more.

Moreover, if you match with a woman you feel enthused about knowing and dating, tell her, and ask her to meet you for coffee. If she says yes, yippie for you; if she says no, move on; the sea has plenty of fish.

Do not be too trusting

Be aware of yourself and protect your personal information while dating online. When you plan a date, do not give out your personal information such as your physical address, and for the first date make sure you meet at a public place.

Remember that online dating attracts a lot of professional scammers, some who will go as far as agreeing to go out with you but who harbor malicious intent. Be safe at all times.

If you keep in mind these tips and the others we have discussed throughout this section, you should be able to navigate the online dating world with confidence as you work towards turning your matches into offline dates and an eventual partnership with the partner of your dreams.

In the next chapter, we shall discuss the signs that will help you know when you've met your ideal partner.

Chapter 9: The Perfect Match: 5 Signs You've Found Your Ideal Partner

As you navigate through online dating, you will no doubt interact with some fantastic women that will "sweep you off your feet" and be contenders for the title of "The One".

Considering that a large percentage of long-term romantic relationships —according to research, **as much as 1 in every five romantic relationships**— now start online, as you interact with your matches online and go on offline dates, you need to keep a keen eye out for signs that may indicate that you have met or found your ideal partner.

In this chapter, we will describe five of these signs:

#: Consistent communication

The online dating world is a strange place — more bizarre than bizarre foods.

One minute you could be talking to and hitting it off with an amazing woman with whom you have a great connection, matching interests and quirkiness, and fantastic chemistry, and the next moment she poofs and disappears on you for weeks on end only to come back and continue the conversation as if she never left. While sad, such scenarios are common.

When you meet an ideal partner, one of the things you will notice about her is that her communication with you will be consistent from the start. She may not be online or available to chat with you all the time, but still, her contact will be regular, and she will not "ghost you".

Consistent communication will tell you that you are probably the only person she is talking to or that she likes you enough to care about talking to you; both are good signs that you may be on to something here.

#: It's the little things that count

Has she commented about how she looks forward to telling you about her day? Does she send you silly jokes, memes, and GIFs because "she wants to brighten your day" and talk to you? How about wanting to tell you about her day at work or the funny thing that happened to her while she was standing in line at the grocery store?

How about you? Do you long to tell her about a fantastic song you heard over the radio, the entertaining thing your coworker related, or an exciting work-related project you are on right now?

If you both feel a desire to share mundane, seemingly trivial details of your life, the chances are high that you have found your ideal partner, because being in love and together is about wanting to share the little things. If she is the first person that comes to mind when something fascinating happens to you, you have found your ideal mate.

#: Openness

Good relationships are about genuine connections. A sincere connection can be many things. A spirit of open sharing is one of its most critical characteristics.

If you notice how you communicate openly with her and she with you about things you usually feel uncomfortable talking about with other people, you may have found your dream girlfriend because ideal partnerships are about open communication and a desire to share things we would never share with other people.

#: You think about her most of the time (if not all the time)

One straightforward way to determine if you have found your "partner in crime" is to notice how often you think about her.

If you think about her often, even when you are not engaging with her actively, you may have found the one. A **2005 research study** concluded that relationships that have "a deep connection" are often devoid of the out-of-sight/out-of-mind phenomena mainly because thinking of her will light up your reward centers and trigger the brain to release feel-good hormones such as dopamine.

#: You support and encourage each other

Dr. John Gottman, a psychology researcher, clinician, and author of various bestselling books on relationships, submits that supporting and encouraging each other is a crucial component of healthy, long-term relationships.

If you notice how you share your dreams, talk about how you can work towards making them work, encourage each other as you both work towards your daily and weekly goals, and share supporting sentiments when either of you has had a tiresome or extraordinarily trying day, you may have found your partner.

According to Gottman, encouraging and supporting each other is a sign of emotional investment in each other.

Action step

You are now at the end of the second section of this guidebook.

The various chapters that made up this section have covered all the strategies, tips, and hacks you need to know and use to ensure that you go from no dating profile to a fantastic dating profile that attracts matches, to messaging women the right way, priming them for rapport, attraction, and dates, and the various steps in between these phases.

Again, this information is valuable to you only if you implement it. So, apply what you have learned and experiment with as many of the strategies we have discussed as possible. You will be glad you did!

Section 3

Being Confident and Aware While Dating Online

"Today, if you own a smartphone, you're carrying a 24-7 singles bar in your pocket."

Aziz Ansari

Welcome to the third section of this ultimate online-dating-for-men guidebook.

In this section, we are going to discuss:

- *The secrets to being confident as you navigate the tumultuous, online dating waters.*

- *The most common online dating scams and the red flags to watch out for.*

- *How to overcome various online dating hurdles regardless of whether you are a single parent, in a long-distance partnership with an amazing girl, do not feel attractive or good looking enough, have language barriers, or are dating online when you are middle-aged.*

And so much, much more.

After reading the various chapters that make up this section of the guidebook, you should feel more confident as you use online dating to find your ideal partner. You should also be able to recognize a dating scam by its tell-tale signs and to wade your way through various online dating hurdles with ease.

Chapter 10: Online Dating Confidence and How to Boost it

In this book, we have consistently noted that to achieve success with online dating and with women, one of the many things you need to do is to remain authentic to the person you are and to make sure that this person is the man you introduce to the women you chat with online and meet offline for dates.

To be an authentic man, you need to have an innate degree of self-belief and self-confidence. You need to believe and trust in yourself, and then steadfastly hold firm to the notion that despite how many hurdles you have to go through or challenges you have to battle and triumph over, you have what it takes to achieve success with women and to have a fantastic dating and relationship life.

In addition to being authentic and genuine to who you are, you need to believe in your deservedness of love, to know your worth, and because of being sure of your worth, to believe that you deserve dating and relationship abundance and to find the partner of your dreams.

Why Confidence Matters So Much

Chanté Salick, a relationship and dating coach, says confidence is a primary ingredient whose availability —or lack thereof— determines your online dating success or failure.

She goes on to note that a lack of confidence, especially as you navigate through online dating, changes your approach. When you lack confidence, instead of approaching the undertaking positively, you approach it with a negative narrative playing out in your mind —an *"all the reasons why I suck at online dating"* monologue— which makes experiencing negative online dating experiences more probable.

Coach Chanté further notes that when you approach any form of dating, but especially online dating, with this narrative playing out in your mind, it changes the energy that permeates your online and offline interactions with women and turns it negative. When this happens, you are likely to communicate insecurity, neediness, desperation, and other negative sentiments you do not want the women you date with a long-term commitment in mind to associate with you.

On the other hand, when you are confident and assured, not only of how deserving you are to be with a drop-dead gorgeous girlfriend but also of your ability to charm the pants off such a woman and to have her hanging on your every word, the more attractive, sensual, and balanced you become.

When you are all these things, it is likely to show in how you approach women online and in how you steer your interactions with them. More importantly, the positive energy that comes from feeling balanced, deserving, and capable will manifest in your verbal and nonverbal communication.

Having talked about the importance of being confident as you navigate the world of online dating, and how having confidence improves your chances of finding love online, we shall turn our attention to how to cultivate it.

3 Simple Ways to Boost Your Dating Confidence

To improve your dating confidence:

#: Cultivate self-awareness

Matching, starting conversations with strangers, and then planning dates with these strangers after a couple of "nice online conversations" is a nerve-wracking experience that can bring up all sorts of fearsome emotions.

If you are not aware of yourself, and of the fears and negative emotions stirred up by the prospect of starting conversations with strangers, you will be akin to an untrained, blindfolded archer.

Work towards being more self-aware so that you can notice when your inner critic flares up in time to quiet it before the fears it causes mutate into a loathsome, impossible-to-slay beast. The more you know yourself and your fears, preconceptions, and negative beliefs, the easier it will be to notice when you start sabotaging your chances of being with a great woman or finding love.

#: Prioritize yourself

Compromises are an integral part of building successful relationships. However, in a world where you are competing against a million other men that are just as eager to have the attention and love of the woman of your dreams, it is easy to go overboard and end up compromising on the things that make you who you are and that bring you great joy in the world.

As you navigate the online dating scene, remember that confidence comes from feeling happy and good about yourself. The best way to instill this sense of wellbeing into your psyche is to prioritize doing things that make you happy.

Do not let things such as rejection, negative conversations with women, "ghosting," and bad dates define who you are as a person. Take everything in stride and remember to do the things you love not with or for the women you date, but for yourself. Pledge that for every five dates you go on with online matches, you will treat yourself to a solo date where you do something you love.

#: Swipe, match, message, meet, repeat

Are you ready for a bare-knuckled truth bomb? Here it is:

We can reduce online dating into five steps: *Swipe, match, message, meet, repeat*. That is all there is to it!

Internalize this simple five-step process, and whenever things fail to go your way –when a woman you were "vibing" with and immensely interested in ghosts you, or your matches unceremoniously un-match you, or you have a date from hell– recall it and remember that no matter what happens, you can use these steps as many times as you want until you find your ideal partner. Do not turn a few failures into a big deal; instead, "swipe, match, message, meet, repeat"!

Beyond all this, the best way to stay grounded and confident as you navigate the busy streets of online dating is to keep things in perspective. Do not idealize or idolize women; no matter how beautiful a woman is, remember that she is human and, therefore, as flawed as you are.

Knowing about the various dating scams and challenges you are likely to encounter as you move through this process will also boost your confidence.

Chapter 11: 3 Online Dating Scams and The Red Flags You Must Never Ignore

Scams have been part of dating since the 1800s when Tillie Marshall used personal ads to swindle men out of their hard-earned money to fund her globe-trotting lifestyle.

Online dating has made scams easier to pull off. In the same breath, it has also made it easier to know which red flags to turn your attention on to avoid falling prey to these scams.

The purpose of this chapter is to give you a list of the three most common dating scams and show you how to recognize and avoid them:

#: Phony dating sites

Because we live in a world of phishing where hackers are eager beavers who want nothing more than to gain access to your private information such as passwords, usernames, and credit card information, phony dating websites are as plentiful as the sands of the ocean. To stay safe, you have to be aware of them.

The best way to avoid phony dating sites is to use the trusted dating platforms we discussed in an earlier part of this guide.

The best way to recognize phony sites is to look out for spoofing signals, digital certificates —fake dating sites usually lack a trusted certificate— and a persistent request for personal information that goes beyond the scope of dating, such as your first school, the street you grew up on, or mother's maiden name.

#: The hard come-on

In a hard come-on scam, shortly after you match and start chatting, the person is likely to declare how much "in love" they are with you, how much they have been "waiting for you all their life", or "how you complete them". Such a person is also likely to want to get you off the dating app as quickly as possible by asking for your social media handles or email address.

To avoid such scams, be self-aware and whenever a match starts professing her love for you or giving you endearing pet names shortly after matching with you, run for the hills.

To recognize such scams, look out for red flags such as declarations of love shortly after matching, lousy grammar, and a hasty desire to move the conversation off the dating app/platform.

#: Dating bots

In the dating bot scam, computer programmers create scripts that create dating profiles whose intent is to interact with you, send messages, and drive the conversation towards tricking you into slipping up and revealing sensitive financial information such as your credit card details. The best way to avoid such scams is to appraise the conversation.

When you are chatting with a bot, it will quickly try to send you off to a third-party website or app that asks for personal information. A bot scam also uses internet photographs and low-quality images as profile photos. If a Google Image search returns conflicting results, it may be possible that the woman you think is "the one" is just a bot.

Dating scams are like chameleons: they change color often. However, like chameleons, even though they can change color, they cannot change their core DNA. If you are aware, keen, and intuitive enough, you should be able to tell when an interaction with someone you met online does not feel right no matter what "color" the communication takes.

The internet also has a lot of information on the various forms of online dating scams and stories —and practical advice on how to stay safe and avoid such scams— from people who have endured such ordeals.

Below are several such resources you can use:

http://zsk.cm/2ELuroj

https://bit.ly/34ObJas

https://bit.ly/2Qizv96

https://bit.ly/2SkMB8t

https://bit.ly/35UyF9o

https://bit.ly/2ZjaHBU

To stay safe from dating scams and scammers, follow the advice we have discussed in this book —the various dos and don'ts of online dating— and do not share personal information. Also, avoid sending anyone money, and meeting at secluded spots.

In the next chapter, we shall discuss how to overcome various online dating hurdles.

Chapter 12: You Can Do This; Overcoming Online- Dating Hurdles

This chapter aims to outline the most common online-dating hurdles and their solutions.

Five Single-Parent Dating Hurdles

Here are five of the most common single-parent dating challenges and how to overcome them:

Hurdle	How to overcome it
Knowing if you are ready, or if it's the right time to start dating	Instead of asking whether you are ready to date, ask yourself why you want to start dating and the needs you think dating will fulfill. If you desire to date because you want to fill a void, you are not ready.
Finding the time to care for your kids and to date	Juggling parenting and dating, especially in the modern world,

	is not easy. Once you decide to give dating a try, find time for it by scheduling it. Ask friends and family to babysit as you treat yourself to a date.
How much to reveal about your present circumstance	Even though it adds a new element to the dating mix, being a single parent is not a crime. Do not treat it as such or try to hide your kids. Be upfront and genuine about what you have going on. Remember that you can find someone amazing, but to do so, you have to be honest.
Unsolicited, negative advice from well-meaning friends and family members	Do not listen to anyone that tells you single parents cannot find love; they can. Believe in yourself and be confident in your ability to use online dating to find your ideal partner.
When to tell the kids about your new, exciting relationship	Take your time before clueing in the kids. Only tell them when you are sure where the relationship with your new "significant other" is heading.

If you adhere to these tips, you should have no trouble overcoming the most common single parents dating hurdles.

2: Long-distance Online Romances

Long-distance relationships are challenging, yes, but with the right approach, you can have a thriving long-distance relationship.

Here are common long-distance relationship hurdles and how to overcome them:

Hurdle	How to overcome it
Miscommunication/lack of communication	The best way to overcome miscommunication, which is the most common of all long-distance relationship hurdles, is open communication. Do not bottle up your feelings. Instead, talk about them openly with each other.
Jealousy	Accept that feeling jealous, especially since your partner is so far away and you cannot see what she is doing, is OK. However, do not give the monster a chance to wash over you. Communicate openly with your partner about what you feel so that you can work through the issue together.

Loneliness	To avoid the loneliness that often creeps into a long-distance online relationship, use modern technology to your advantage. Message each other often and video-chat or call at least once per day. The more you stay connected to your partner, the less lonely you will feel.

Keep these hurdles —and their solutions— in mind as you use online dating, especially if you are dating someone outside your city, state, or even country.

3: Unattractive/Not Good-Looking Enough

Online dating is very physical-appearance-driven because of the swiping nature of dating apps. If you do not feel attractive or good-looking enough, this can pose a challenge.

Here are the most common dating hurdles you are likely to experience when you feel unattractive/not handsome enough and how to overcome them:

Hurdle	How to overcome it
How to put your best "face" forward in your profile picture	To "put your best face forward", the best thing to do is to go with a witty but honest picture. Do not try to photoshop a beautiful face onto your body. You cannot go wrong with an action shot, or a photograph of you immersed in something you love doing.
What to say about yourself on your dating bio	Remember that a dating profile bio is not a place to describe your best physical attributes. It is a place to be authentic about who you are and what makes you tick. Use the space to give women an idea of what you are about without revealing too much.
Struggling to decide which dating app to use	Which dating app you choose to use does not matter much because if you optimize your dating profile, you will (eventually) find someone who loves you for who you are. However, you cannot go wrong with niche dating sites such as **Nerd Passions** and **Geek 2 Geek**.

Remember that "beauty is in the eyes of the beholder". While you may not consider yourself attractive or good-looking enough, you will be all those things (and more) to the right person. All you have to do it stick in there and to keep looking for your dream girlfriend until you find her.

4: Middle-aged Online Dating Hurdles

If you are middle-aged, here are the dating challenges you are likely to encounter —and how to troubleshoot them:

Hurdle	How to overcome it
Confusing language and internet verbiage	To navigate online dating well, you have to learn the lingo and commonly used abbreviations such as LOL (laugh out loud) FWB (friends with benefits), and other such words. When you encounter such words and other unfamiliar ones, Google is your best friend.
Staying safe while using online dating	Middle-aged men (and women) are prime targets for scammers. To ensure your safety, and to avoid falling prey to a scam, do not share personal information, and be very mindful and aware of the nature of conversations with your matches. You can use Google to verify your matches' info (even their images), and when something does not feel right, remember that it is better to be safe than sorry.

| Which dating app to use | You can use any dating app, but for the best results, it is best to use a dating app that specifically caters to singles over 40 like **Lumen** or **OurTime**. |

These tips should help you overcome these three common middle-aged dating hurdles.

How to Overcome Language Barriers in Online Dating

If you decide to date as far outside your comfort zone as possible by dating a woman who speaks a different language, you will deal with language barriers. The best way to deal with language barriers of all types is to use online translation tools and apps and to commit to learning a new language, even if you only learn a few words. You can also use a translator; most trusted intercultural dating platforms offer translation services.

Conclusion

Thank you for reading this guide.

While online dating can feel overwhelming at first, I hope that this book has made the process clearer and easier for you and that you now have an idea of what you need to do to achieve online dating success.

As mentioned repeatedly, what matters the most is not reading this book. Yes, reading the book is important, but implementing what you have learned is the most crucial thing.

Implement and experiment with the numerous online dating tips, strategies, and hacks scattered throughout this guidebook and without a doubt, you will use the internet and dating apps to attract women and get a girlfriend.

Thank you again for reading and good luck on your journey.

Printed in Dunstable, United Kingdom